Boston, Massachusetts, Justin Winsor

Celebration of the Centennial Anniversary of the Battle of Bunker Hill

Boston, Massachusetts, Justin Winsor

Celebration of the Centennial Anniversary of the Battle of Bunker Hill

ISBN/EAN: 9783743686847

Printed in Europe, USA, Canada, Australia, Japan

Cover: Foto ©ninafisch / pixelio.de

More available books at **www.hansebooks.com**

CENTENNIAL ANNIVERSARY

OF THE

BATTLE OF BUNKER HILL.

CITY HALL.

[Drawn by A. R. WAUD. Engraved by A. V. S. ANTHONY.]

CELEBRATION

OF THE

CENTENNIAL ANNIVERSARY

OF THE

BATTLE OF BUNKER HILL.

WITH AN APPENDIX CONTAINING A SURVEY OF THE
LITERATURE OF THE BATTLE, ITS
ANTECEDENTS AND RESULTS.

Boston:
PRINTED BY ORDER OF THE CITY COUNCIL.
MDCCCLXXV.

CITY OF BOSTON.

IN BOARD OF ALDERMEN, June 21, 1875.

ORDERED, That the Clerk of Committees be requested to prepare and print an account of the celebration in this city, commemorative of the centennial anniversary of the battle of Bunker Hill; and that one thousand copies be printed for the use of the City Government, to be distributed under the direction of the Committee on Printing, the expense to be charged to the appropriation for Incidentals.

IN COMMON COUNCIL, July 1, 1875.

Concurred.

Approved July 3d, 1875.

Press of
ROCKWELL AND CHURCHILL,
39 Arch Street, Boston.

CONTENTS.

	PAGE
PRELIMINARY ARRANGEMENTS	9
Mayor's Inaugural Address	12
Report of Special Committee	12
Order of City Council	13
City's Programme	13
City's Invitations	14
Action of the Legislature	15
Circular of Chief Marshal	16–21
Notice of the Chief of Police	21
RECEPTION IN MUSIC HALL	25
The Mayor's Welcome	26–34
Remarks of Gov. Gaston	35
Remarks of Col. A. O Andrews	36–41
Remarks of Gen. Fitz Hugh Lee	41
Remarks of Gen. J. C. Kilpatrick	43
Remarks of Gen. W. T. Sherman	45
Remarks of Gen. A. E. Burnside	46
Remarks of Vice-President Wilson	46
THE PROCESSION	51
The Decorations	51
The Review	52
The Chief Marshal and Staff	52
Massachusetts Volunteer Militia	53
First Division of Procession	55
Second Division of Procession	57
Third Division of Procession	61
Fourth Division of Procession	63
Fifth Division of Procession	64
Sixth Division of Procession	65
Seventh Division of Procession	67
Eighth Division of Procession	68
Ninth Division of Procession	69

	PAGE
SERVICES ON BUNKER HILL	75
Prayer by Rev. Rufus Ellis	76
Hymn — Prayer before Battle	77
Address of Hon. Charles Devens, Jr.	78
Hymn, written by Charles James Sprague	126
Address by Hon. G. Washington Warren	127
Remarks of General Sherman	130
Remarks of Governor Hartranft	132
Song, written by Charles James Sprague	134
Remarks of Governor Bedle	134
Remarks of Governor Dingley	137
Remarks of Vice-President Wilson	138
Despatch from San Francisco	140
Despatch from New Orleans	140
Ode, written by Geo. Sennott	141
Hymn, written by G. Washington Warren	142
Letter from Governor Ingersoll	143
Letter from Mayor of New Orleans	144
Letter from Mayor of Memphis	145
Letter from Mayor of Omaha	146
Despatch from Ladies of Allentown, Pa.	147
Despatch from National Board of Trade	147
APPENDIX: —	
Literature of Bunker Hill, with its antecedents and results	151

PRELIMINARY ARRANGEMENTS.

PRELIMINARY ARRANGEMENTS.

In his inaugural address to the City Council of Boston, on the 5th of January, 1875, the Mayor — Hon. SAMUEL C. COBB — referred to the approaching centennial anniversary in the following words: —

"The centennial epoch of our national history is close at hand. Preparations are now being made to celebrate the hundredth anniversary of the declaration of independence, on a grand scale, in the city from which that momentous document was promulgated. The startling events in Boston and its vicinity, in 1775, aroused the sympathetic patriotism of the sister colonies, and justified and made possible that solemn act of the Continental Congress of 1776. Those events will be commemorated. Our neighbors at Lexington and Concord are preparing for the local celebration of the acts of heroism which have rendered those names famous. The scene of the first great revolutionary combat is now within our municipal limits. The patriotic Association which has charge of the grounds will, doubtless, initiate measures for the due observance of the 17th of June next, the hundredth anniversary of the battle of Bunker Hill. It will be for you to consider to what extent this government can properly co-operate with them."

This portion of the Mayor's address was referred to a joint special committee of the City Council, consisting of Aldermen Thomas B. Harris and Solomon B. Stebbins, Councilmen Edwin Sibley, Eugene H. Sampson and Isaac P. Clarke. The committee reported on the 12th of April, as follows:—

The joint special committee to which was referred so much of the Mayor's inaugural address as relates to the celebration of the 17th of June next, having carefully considered the subject, beg leave to submit the following report:—

The one hundredth anniversary of the first great battle of the American Revolution is an event which clearly calls for recognition and commemorative action on the part of the municipal authorities of Boston; and the only question would seem to be the extent and character of the action which it would be proper, and, under the circumstances, desirable, for the city government to take.

Your committee have conferred with the representatives of the State and of the Bunker Hill Monument Association; but no definite action can be taken until the representatives of the city are duly authorized to give their assent to such arrangements as may be agreed upon for the celebration.

It is proposed, on the part of the State, to invite as its guests the principal executive officers of the United States and governors of the several States; and to order out, for review and for escort duty, the entire militia organization of this State. With a view to secure harmony of action, and prevent confusion in carrying out the details, it is suggested that all the other matters connected with the celebration — except the delivery of the oration, for which arrangements have already been made by the Monument Association — should be under the control and management of the city. On that basis an approximate estimate has been prepared of the expense which the city would be called upon to bear, amounting in the total to thirty thousand dollars, and the committee would respectfully recommend the passage of an order appropriating that amount. . . . . . .

Respectfully submitted,
For the Committee,
THOMAS B. HARRIS,
Chairman.

The following order was passed by the City Council, and approved by the Mayor, on the 7th of May: —

Ordered, That His Honor the Mayor, the Chairman of the Board of Aldermen, the President of the Common Council, with Aldermen Harris, Stebbins, Quincy and Power, and Councilmen Sibley, Sampson, Clarke, Peabody, Flynn, Guild and Devereux, be authorized to make suitable arrangements, on the part of the City of Boston, for the Celebration of the Centennial Anniversary of the Battle of Bunker Hill; and that said committee be authorized to expend for that purpose the income of the Foss fund, and of the Babcock fund, and, in addition thereto, a sum not exceeding thirty thousand dollars,* to be charged to the appropriation for Incidentals.

The Mayor, having been empowered by the committee to select a suitable person to act as Chief Marshal of the procession which it was proposed to organize on the day of the celebration, appointed General FRANCIS A. OSBORN, with full authority to make such arrangements, in matters pertaining to the duties of the office, as he might deem necessary.

The part to be taken by the city in the observance of the anniversary was further defined as follows: It was decided to have an official reception in Music Hall on the evening of the 16th of June; to decorate all the public buildings, and designate, by suitable inscriptions, the places of historical interest in the city; to have the bells of the churches rung, and national salutes fired at sunrise, noon and sunset, on the 17th; to provide a tent and such other accommodations as may be necessary for the exercises at Bunker Hill; to make a display of fireworks on Boston Common and on Sullivan square, in Charlestown; to illuminate the dome of the City Hall, in School street, and the front and dome of the old City Hall, in Charlestown; to exhibit calcium lights from the top of

---

* On the 5th of June this sum was increased to $35,000. The amount actually expended was $33,414.46.

the Bunker Hill Monument, and from other prominent points in the city proper, and in East Boston, South Boston and Roxbury; and to have bonfires in Dorchester, West Roxbury and Brighton.

By request of the committee, the Mayor extended a cordial invitation to the following-named officials to accept the hospitalities of the city: —

The Mayor of Mobile, Ala.; Little Rock, Ark.; San Francisco, Cal.; New Haven, Conn.; Wilmington, Del.; Jacksonville, Fla.; Savannah, Ga.; Chicago, Ill.; Indianapolis, Ind.; Davenport, Iowa; Leavenworth, Kansas; Louisville, Ky.; New Orleans, La.; Portland, Me.; Baltimore, Md.; Detroit, Mich.; St. Paul, Minn.; Vicksburg, Miss.; St. Louis, Mo.; Omaha, Neb.; Virginia, Nevada; Manchester, N. H.; Newark, N. J.; New York, N. Y.; Wilmington, N. C.; Cincinnati, Ohio; Portland, Oregon; Philadelphia, Pa.; Providence, R. I.; Charleston, S. C.; Memphis, Tenn.; Galveston, Texas; Burlington, Vt.; Richmond, Va.; Wheeling, W. Va.; Milwaukee, Wis.; General Joseph R. Hawley, President U. S. Centennial Commission; Alfred T. Goshorn, Esquire, Director General U. S. Centennial Commission; Honorable John Welch, President of the Board of Finance, U. S. Centennial Commission; Frederick Fraley, Esquire, Secretary and Treasurer of the Board of Finance, U. S. Centennial Commission; Honorable William Bigler, Financial Agent U. S. Centennial Commission; Honorable Daniel J. Morrell, Chairman Executive Committee U. S. Centennial Commission.

The following persons were invited to meet the Mayor at the City Hall, at 9 o'clock on the morning of the 17th, for the purpose of uniting with the City Government in the exercises of the day: —

The Mayors of cities in Massachusetts; the past Mayors of

Boston, Roxbury and Charlestown; Hon. E. R. Hoar, Mr. Ralph Waldo Emerson, and Mr. George Heywood, committee of the town of Concord; Mr. Charles Hudson, Mr. M. H. Merriam, and Mr. W. H. Munroe, committee of the town of Lexington; Prof. Charles W. Eliot, President of Harvard College; Hon. Charles Francis Adams, Mr. Henry W. Longfellow, Mr. James Russell Lowell, Dr. O. W. Holmes, Mr. William Gray, Mr. Wendell Phillips, Mr. William Lloyd Garrison, and others.

Under an order of the House of Representatives, passed the 13th of March, a joint special committee of the Massachusetts Legislature was appointed, "with full power to make such arrangements as might be deemed proper and expedient for the reception, on the part of the State, of the President and Vice-President of the United States, and other distinguished strangers who might visit the State upon the occasion of the celebration of the 17th of June."

The committee subsequently invited the following persons to become the guests of the State: The President and Vice-President of the United States; the President *pro tempore* of the United States Senate; the Speaker of the House of Representatives of the United States; the members of the President's Cabinet; the Judges of the Supreme Judicial Court of the United States; General William T. Sherman; Lieutenant General Philip H. Sheridan; Major General Winfield S. Hancock; Admiral David D. Porter; Vice-Admiral Stephen C. Rowan; the Governors of all the States; the Chiefs of the Diplomatic Corps; the Senators and Representatives in Congress from Maine; Andrew Johnson, Ex-President of the United States; and John A. Dix, of New York.

On the 14th of June His Excellency, the Governor and Commander-in-Chief, tendered the First Division of Massachusetts Volunteer Militia to the City of Boston, for the purpose of escort duty at the Centennial Anniversary, and stated, at the same time, that the troops would pass in review at the State House, while *en route* to the head of the civic procession.

In response to a request from the Mayor, Major General W. S. Hancock, commanding the Military Division of the Atlantic, directed Major George P. Andrews, of the Fifth U. S. Artillery, to detail two companies from the troops in Boston Harbor, under the command of Brevet Major General Richard Arnold, to report for duty, in connection with the procession.

In a circular* issued just previous to the 17th, the Chief Marshal made the following announcement in regard to the formation and management of the procession, and the route over which it would pass: —

The First Division Massachusetts Volunteer Militia has been ordered by the Major General commanding to form upon the Parade Ground of the Common at 8.40, A. M. Before reporting for duty as escort of the procession, the division is to march in review before the Governor and Commander-in-Chief, who is to take post for the purpose in front of the State House. The column of troops is to move from the Parade Ground through Boylston-street mall, Tremont, Beacon, and Dartmouth streets. It is to halt in Dartmouth street, the right resting at Columbus avenue, and is to close in mass, thus assuming position to take up the procession.

The procession, except the First Division, will form at 10 o'clock in the several positions named below.

The First Division will form at 9 o'clock in Charles street, the right resting at Boylston street, the left prolonged toward Beacon street, and up Beacon-street mall. This division, in conformity with the wish of its constituent bodies and of the State authorities, will join in the march in review, and will follow the division of Massachusetts Militia. When that division shall close in mass and halt, the First Division will close upon it and execute the same movement.

* The circular gave the organization of the several divisions; but that portion is omitted here, as it is given more in detail in the account of the procession.

The official personages composing the Second Division will witness the review at the State House. The several escorts to Governors of States will be posted as follows: The First Troop of City Cavalry, of Philadelphia, in Ashburton place, right resting at Bowdoin street. The First Company Governor's Foot Guards, of Hartford, escort of the Governor of Connecticut, the Portland Cadets, escort of the Governor of Maine, and the Governor Straw Rifles, escort of the Governor of New Hampshire, in the Park-street mall, right resting at Beacon street. The National Lancers, escort of the State Government, in Derne street, right resting at Bowdoin street. Immediately after the review, the chief of this division will exert himself to form it as speedily as possible. The City Government and their guests will leave the State House by the door on Mount Vernon street, will take their carriages and drive rapidly to Charles street, where they will form, the right resting at Beacon street, the left prolonged toward Cambridge street. The State Government and their guests will leave the State House by the Beacon-street side, will take their carriages, and, preceded by the Lancers, will drive down Beacon street, and form with the right resting at Charles street, in position to follow the City Government. The escorts will be moved up in season to take up their respective Governors in their proper places.

The Third Division will form on Beacon street, the right resting at Dartmouth street, the left prolonged toward Parker street.

The Fourth Division will form on Marlboro' street, the right resting at Dartmouth street, the left prolonged toward Arlington street.

The Fifth Division will form on Marlboro' street, the right resting at Dartmouth street, the left prolonged toward Parker street.

The Sixth Division will form on Commonwealth avenue, north side, the right resting at Dartmouth street, the left prolonged toward Arlington street.

The Seventh Division will form in two subdivisions, the first on Commonwealth avenue, south side, and the second on Newbury street, the right of each subdivision resting at Dartmouth street, the left prolonged toward Arlington street. The Chief of this division will detail an Aid to see that the second subdivision moves promptly to unite with the first.

The Eighth Division will form on Boylston street, the right resting at Dartmouth street, the left prolonged toward Arlington street.

The Ninth Division will form on Chandler and Appleton streets, Warren avenue, Brookline, Pembroke, Newton, Rutland and Concord streets, or as many of them as may be needed, in the order named, — the right of the subdivisions in Brookline and Pembroke streets, resting at Warren avenue; the right of those in the other streets named, resting at Columbus avenue. All wagons will enter the designated streets at the rear, and will be formed in single column from front to rear, in the order of their reporting, excepting those bearing very unwieldy loads, and liable for that reason to delay the march, which will be posted at the rear of the division. A line will first be formed in Chandler street, close by the northern curbstone, and a second line close by the southern curbstone; and the same order will be followed in the other streets. The line first formed will move first, and the second will follow close in its rear. Teams of more than a single pair of horses will be provided with men to walk beside the leaders, as security against accident and delay. Wagons heavily loaded must be furnished with brakes.

The head-quarters of the Chief Marshal will be at the corner of Beacon and Arlington streets. The General Staff will report to him there at 9 o'clock, A.M.

Chiefs of Divisions will establish their head-quarters at the points indicated above for the right of their respective divisions, and will remain, or be represented there, until their divisions shall move. They will detail bearers for the respective division banners, who will be stationed, during the formation, at the right of the division, and who will march in advance of the division, thirty paces in rear of the one preceding. They will also detail mounted orderlies, to carry their respective head-quarter flags. Each Chief of Division, when he shall see the division next preceding his own in motion, will close his division in mass, and be prepared to march promptly, at an interval of thirty paces in its rear; he will station an Aid at the rear of his division, to notify the Chief of the succeeding one of the moment to move. Each Chief of Division will labor during the march to maintain his division at the prescribed interval; and, if he shall find that it is losing distance, or becoming unduly extended, he will at once communicate the fact to the Chief Marshal.

Divisions, in taking up the line of march, will take distance by the head of column.

Aids detailed by the Chief Marshal will attend at the several railroad stations for the purpose of giving all necessary information to organizations arriving. They will reach the stations at 9, A.M., and remain until 11, A.M. Organizations are requested to follow the route from the railroad station which may be indicated by such Aids.

As each organization arrives on the ground prescribed for its division, its Chief will report at once to the Chief of Division the total number of its members present, of its band, and of its carriages, and it will be assigned a place in column.

All but military bodies will form and march in single ranks of six files each. Carriages will form two abreast, and maintain that order during the march.

The formation of the procession cannot be completed until after the conclusion of the military review. After the troops, and the official personages who will be present at the review, shall have taken their respective positions, the head of the column will take up the line of march, at an hour not earlier than 11½ o'clock, from the corner of Dartmouth street and Columbus avenue, and will move through the following-named streets: —

Columbus avenue, West Chester park, Chester square, southwest side, Washington and Union Park streets, Union park, southwest side, Tremont, Boylston, Washington, Milk, India, Commercial and South Market streets, Merchants' row, State, Devonshire, Washington and Charlestown streets, Charles-river bridge, Charles-river avenue, City square, Chelsea, Chestnut, southeast and northeast sides of Monument square, Concord, Bunker Hill and Main streets, Monument avenue, southwest side of Monument square and Winthrop street to Winthrop square, where the procession will be dismissed.

While crossing all bridges, bands and drums will cease playing and marching bodies will break step. Chiefs of Division will impress upon their commands the importance of this order, and will labor to enforce it, leaving an Aid at the entrance of each bridge for the purpose.

The Chief Marshal has secured a line of telegraph along the whole route, and has established stations at the following places:—

No. 1. Corner Beacon and Arlington streets, head-quarters Chief Marshal.
No. 2. Corner Dartmouth street and Columbus avenue.
No. 3. Corner Chester square and Washington street.
No. 4. 5th Police Station, East Dedham street.
No. 5. 282 Tremont street, corner Common street.
No. 6. No. 411 Washington street, at Haley, Morse & Co.'s store.
No. 7. Milk street, near Broad street.
No. 8. Old State House.
No. 9. Haymarket square, in or near Boston and Maine Railroad depot.
No. 10. City square, Charlestown.
No. 11. Main, corner Thorndike street.
No. 12. Winthrop square, opposite Park street.

Chiefs of Division, on approaching each station, will send forward an Aid, with the despatch for the Chief Marshal, giving full information of the condition of their commands, and any other matters deemed by them important. They will instruct their Aids to receive any orders which may be waiting delivery.

The operators at these stations will from time to time exhibit placards, for the information of the spectators, announcing the position of the head of the column.

Any Chief of Division not ready to move promptly in his order will at once notify the Chief of the one next succeeding, to march in his place and stead, and will take position for the march in rear of the last marching division, retaining at the head of his own its proper banner. Should he, however, be subject to detention by the unreadiness of a small portion of his command, he may, at his discretion, detach such portion, and send it, under charge of an Aid, to report to the Chief of the last marching division.

Any organization reaching the ground after the departure of its division will report to the Chief of the next succeeding one, not already in motion.

Chiefs of Division are requested to transmit to these head-quarters, on the day following the celebration, consolidated reports of their commands.

By order of GEN. FRANCIS A. OSBORN,
Chief Marshal.

CORNELIUS G. ATTWOOD, *Adjutant General.*

In connection with the Marshal's notice, the Chief of Police issued the following: —

By direction of the BOARD OF ALDERMEN, the streets designated by the Chief Marshal as the route for the procession on the 17th of June, and such other streets as the public safety and convenience may require, will be closed against the passage of vehicles at 9 o'clock, A. M.

The streets adjacent to the Common, and those on the Back Bay Territory on which the procession is to be formed, will be closed against the passage of vehicles at 8 o'clock, A. M.

Monument square and (west) Monument avenue will be closed against the passage of vehicles at 8 o'clock, A. M., and against the passage of all persons not authorized to pass there at 8 o'clock, A. M., on that day.

All unnecessary obstructions on the streets or sidewalks must be removed, and it is highly desirable that all persons should aid the police in securing an unobstructed passage, from curb to curb, throughout the entire route of the procession.

For rates of hack-fares between Boston proper and Charlestown passengers are directed to the list of fares posted in each carriage.

The law against the discharge of firearms and fireworks will be promptly enforced, and all citizens are earnestly requested not to leave their dwellings unprotected, and to use every practical precaution against fire.

EDWARD H. SAVAGE,
Chief of Police.

OFFICE OF THE CHIEF OF POLICE,
Boston, June 14, 1875.

THE RECEPTION IN MUSIC HALL.

RECEPTION IN MUSIC HALL.

[Drawn by EDWIN A. ABBEY   Engraved by A. V. S. ANTHONY.]

THE RECEPTION IN MUSIC HALL.

On the evening of the 16th of June His Honor the Mayor and the Committee of Arrangements gave a reception, in Music Hall, to the distinguished visitors who purposed taking part in the celebration on the following day.

The hall was very handsomely decorated with flowers, bunting and drapery. On the front of the upper balcony there was an arch bearing the word "WELCOME," in richly illuminated letters; and, just beneath, a representation of the City Seal, with the dates "1775" and "1875," in tablets on either side. At intervals during the evening music was furnished by the Germania Band.

To facilitate the interchange of civilities between the city authorities and their guests, the seats in the body of the hall were removed; and to accommodate the ladies, a portion of the seats in the first balcony were reserved. Among those who occupied seats on the platform, or who appeared there at different times during the evening, there were, the Vice-President of the United States, General William T. Sherman, Senator Ambrose E. Burnside; Mr. Justice Strong of the Supreme Court, U. S.; Señor Don Francisco Gonzales Errazuriz, Chargé d'Affaires from Chili; Mr. Stephen Preston, Envoy Extraordinary and Minister Plenipotentiary from Hayti; His Excellency William Gaston, Governor of Massachusetts; His Excellency Nelson Dingley, Jr., Governor of Maine; His Excellency John J. Bagley, Governor of Michigan; General Fitz Hugh Lee, of Virginia; Colonel A. O. Andrews, of South Carolina, Captain J. W.

Gilmer, of the Norfolk Blues; General Judson C. Kilpatrick; Hon. R. W. Richardson, Mayor of Portland; Hon. R. L. Fulton, Mayor of Galveston, Texas. Among the organizations, or representatives of organizations, present in the hall there were, the Washington Light Infantry of Charleston, S. C.; the Norfolk Light Artillery Blues, of Norfolk, Va.; the Fifth Maryland Regiment; the Old Guard of New York; the Light Infantry Veteran Association of Salem, Mass.; the New England Society of New York; the Richmond (Va.) Commandery of Knights Templars; the De Molay Commandery of Boston; The Ancient and Honorable Artillery Company of Boston, and the Bunker Hill Monument Association.

Soon after eight o'clock the Mayor called the assemblage to order, and spoke as follows: —

THE MAYOR'S WELCOME.

Fellow-Citizens and Friends: — The event whose hundredth anniversary we celebrate to-morrow was one of a series that resulted in the creation of an independent nation. The battle of Bunker Hill, in a military view, was a defeat for the colonies; but, in its moral and political fruits, it was a splendid success. Following close upon the collisions at Lexington and Concord, it fired the whole American heart, and aroused the entire American people, and made them thenceforth one people. While it fell to the lot of Massachusetts to lead off in the war of independence, she was not left to stand alone for a day. Responses of sympathy and pledges of co-operation came in as fast as news could fly and men could march.

"It is surprising," writes General Gage at this period, "that so many of the other provinces interest themselves so much in this. They have warm friends in New York, and I learn that the people of Charleston, South Carolina, are as mad as they are here."

"All Virginia," says Irving, "was in a state of combustion."

"We must fight!" said Patrick Henry. "I repeat it, sir, we must fight!"

In fifteen days the great Virginian, Washington himself, was here at the head of the army. Then followed battle after battle, from Boston to Charleston, from Saratoga to Yorktown, till at length the thirteen provinces became thirteen States, and those thirteen States an empire that now spans the continent. Remembering these things, we of the East do more than willingly accord to the people of the West and the South an equal share in the proud and grateful memories that belong to our revolutionary centennials ; and we, on our part, shall claim an equal share in theirs, as they recur from time to time, from '75 to '82.

To-morrow's commemoration is no mere local affair. It must have a national significance, or it can have none. If it were only Boston or Massachusetts, or even New England, that cared for it, better that the famous story of Bunker Hill were blotted out of history, as the mere record of an ignominious failure. What is ours in these things belongs to all our countrymen as much, or it would be worthless to us ; and what is theirs is ours, or we should feel bereft of a splendid heritage. It is, therefore, with the deepest satisfaction that we, who are especially at home here, hail the coming of so many of our fellow-citizens from abroad and afar. Their presence is a principal circumstance, and, to our eyes, the brightest feature of the occasion — a pledge that they are ready to share, and share alike with us, in the rich inheritance of the inspiring memories and traditions of the national birthtime, and that to their feeling, as to ours, the sons of their fathers and of our fathers, who stood shoulder to shoulder in that grand old time, are, and must be, brethren to-day.

Under the inspirations of such a reunion, we feel that to-morrow will be such a red-letter day for Boston as can hardly shine for her more than once in a century. If the skies smile upon her there will be such a tide of life pulsing through her streets as she never knew before; her spires and domes will wear such a radiance as the summer sun never gave them till now; the heart of Bunker Hill will throb audibly beneath the tread and the acclaim of the gathering multitudes; its granite shaft will loom up many cubits taller into the sky; and the glorified forms of Prescott and Warren, and of their illustrious compeers who stood with them on the spot that day, or who sent them their sympathy, and were already hastening to their support from every quarter, or preparing to do the like deeds elsewhere, will almost be seen bending from the clouds and breathing benedictions on their children, who, after all the vicissitudes of a century, are found faithful to their trust, and worthy to hold and transmit their sacred inheritance of liberty and union. Under these circumstances the City Council, acting as they felt, and sure that it was in accord with the sentiment of the whole city, have desired me to invite our visitors to meet us here to-night for an interchange of greetings and felicitations.

We knew you were coming, gentlemen; and you have come as you promised, and as we hoped — in goodly numbers — in military, masonic, industrial, commercial and educational organizations — private citizens and representatives of the Nation, of the States and of many cities. You have come from every direction and all distances; from beyond the Kennebec and the Green Mountains; from beyond the Hudson, the Delaware and the Susquehanna, the Potomac and the James, the Edisto, the Savannah and the Tennessee; from beyond the Mississippi and the Rocky Mountains. You could not come too numerously for our wishes and our welcome. Boston would be glad if she could fold the whole nation in her heart to-morrow, and make herself for the day, and in this her turn, the sacred Mecca of the entire American people. Without dissent or reservation she rejoices as one man in your coming; and in her name and behalf I bid you welcome! — thrice welcome! — a thousand times welcome! My clumsy northern tongue and unpractised lips cannot give adequate expression to the warmth and cordiality with which she bids me greet her guests and make them at home within her gates. And, if I mistake not, the crowds in our streets to-morrow will re-echo the greeting with an emphasis that you cannot fail to understand. You will unite with us, and that right heartily, I doubt not, in commemorating with reverence and gratitude the men and the deeds of a hundred years ago, and the ways in which an ever gracious Providence, through many perils and difficulties, has led our country on and up to its present height of greatness and prosperity.

And now, fellow-citizens, while we solemnly ring out the old century, let us hopefully ring in the new. It belongs to the men of to-day to inaugurate the second century of our country's life. The omens are propitious. The prospects of our national polity are brighter to-day, I think, than at any previous period. It has safely undergone all the tests that could be crowded into a century. It still stands, and may now be said to have almost passed the experimental stage,— at least as far as that can be said of any earthly polity. We have experienced all the trials and dangers by which the permanence of nations is put to the test. We have had the stringent test of unexampled prosperity and rapid expansion, and have survived it. We have had commercial crises and industrial depressions of the severest character. We have had bitter political and sectional strifes. We have had foreign wars; and, like all nations that have attained to greatness, we have had civil war,— and still we live. This last and supremest peril has passed away just in time to enable the country to enter upon the second century of its history with confidence and good cheer. We could not have said so, at least not so confidently, fifteen years ago, nor ten, nor even five. But now, not only is the war closed, but the animosities which have accompanied and followed it are fading out; they are dying,— nay, they are as good as dead, and awaiting their burial! To-morrow we will dig their grave; at the greater centennial in Philadelphia, next year, we will heap up a mound over them high as the Alleghanies; and, before the day of Yorktown comes round, we shall have forgotten that they ever existed.

In this benign work of reconciliation the soldiers on both sides have taken the lead. This was to be expected. True heroism harbors no resentments, and is incapable of a sullen and persistent hatred. True soldiers, worthy of the name, give and take hard blows in all honor and duty; and when the work is done, are ready to embrace as brothers in arms, and to let by-gones be by-gones, in all things except to preserve the memory and decorate the graves of their heroic dead,—ay, and of one another's dead. Brave men love brave men, with the magnanimity that knows how to honor each other's courage and respect each other's motives. Foemen in war, brothers in peace;—that is the history of chivalry here, as everywhere. And all classes must needs follow the lead of their noble champions, and could not stand out against it, if they would. Even the weak and cowardly, and the political adventurers who live on the garbage of sectional jealousies and partisan embitterments, have to give in, at last, from very shame. Indications of the spreading and deepening of this sentiment of restored amity are coming in from all quarters. Here in Boston, I do not happen to know a single voice at variance with it; and that it is shared by yourselves, gentlemen of the South, is evidenced by your presence here to-night. You may have desired the issue of the war to have been other than it is, and may have felt, for a time, that all was lost save honor. I respect your convictions; but I believe you are wise enough, and magnanimous enough, to acquiesce loyally now, and in the end cheerfully, in the arbitrament of the God of battles, — assured, as you must be, that the overruling Providence is wiser than our wishes, and knows how to bestow richer benefits than those it withholds; assured, too, that whatever was right and good in the lost cause which you loved is not finally lost, and that whatever was false or wrong in the winning cause cannot permanently triumph. The Almighty reigns, and shapes results more beneficently and more righteously than man can.

All things considered, fellow-citizens, I regard our country as prepared to enter upon its second century with the best auguries and brightest hopes of peace and happiness. The burdens and privations resulting from the cost and the waste of war, on both sides, we must still bear for a time, as we are bearing them now, in this universal depression of industry and trade. But this evil is, in its nature, transient for a vigorous and thrifty people, and need count but little in our reckoning on the future, provided only that harmony and mutual confidence and good-will prevail and continue. And these we must foster and defend. All depends on these. I am sure you will agree with me, gentlemen, that in the new century there need not be, and must not be, any North, or South, or East, or West, except in respect to those varieties of climate and production which stimulate industry, and give life to commerce, and multiply the sources of national wealth and power. While we cultivate friendly relations by the intercourse of trade and the amenities of social life, we must avoid the political intermeddling that endangers such relations. Let each State manage its own local affairs without interference, however well meant, from abroad, subject only to that Constitution which is at once a wholesome restraint and a protecting shield for us all.

The old political issues have well-nigh passed away; one platform is very much like another. Old party lines are getting mixed and shadowy, so that little remains to distinguish them but their names. We are thus at liberty to seek the best men as rulers, without reference to party or locality, or anything but character and capacity, — honest men, who will neither steal nor permit stealing. The securing of a pure and upright government would be the best fruit of our restored harmony, and the best inauguration I know of for the new century. Let good men, in all sections, combine as one man for this end. There must still be parties, with or without the old names, — sharp antagonisms of opinion and policy. These are everywhere among the conditions of freedom and progress. They do not destroy, they invigorate, a nation. The only fatal divisions are those of sections. There must be none of these, — at least in that part of the century which our lifetime shall cover, and for which we are answerable. No conflict of sections! I give you my hand on that proposition, gentlemen, and I promise you every honest man's hand in Boston on that. And, if you will accept and return the pledge, it shall be kept; and we may trust our children and our children's children to maintain and perpetuate it. We must guard against the beginnings of alienation and distrust; and, if ever we see any root of bitterness giving signs of springing up, let us set our heels upon it, yours and ours, and stamp it out before it has time to send up a single poison-shoot.

But I detain you too long, gentlemen. Much formal address is not what we want to-night. We want rather to look into one another's faces, eye to eye. We want to give and take a hearty hand-grasp. We want to tell you, collectively and individually, that we shall be but too ready and glad to do all in our power to make your visit agreeable to you, and to convince you that the confidence in us which you show by coming is not misplaced. We want to enable you to report to your people at home that you found nothing but brotherhood and good-fellowship here. We want to make the guests of a week the friends of a lifetime. We want you to feel as kindly towards Boston as Boston does towards your own fair cities of the South, to whom God grant health and wealth, prosperity and peace!

Once more, to all our guests, from far away and from near by, and from all points of the compass, I say in the city's name, and say it gratefully and heartily, Welcome to Boston and Bunker Hill!

The Mayor's remarks were warmly applauded. After music by the band, he presented Governor GASTON, who spoke as follows:—

REMARKS OF GOVERNOR GASTON.

Mr. Mayor, Ladies and Gentlemen: — My words will be few to-night; but I should poorly represent Massachusetts, as her heart now beats, if they were not charged with the warmest spirit of welcome.

Massachusetts is honored by the presence of the sons and daughters of all the States who have come here from every part of this broad land to honor the memory of the soldiers and the statesmen who laid the foundations of a republic which now numbers forty millions of people.

The early battles of the Revolution were fought on Massachusetts soil, but they were not fought for Massachusetts alone. They were fought for the entire country, and the glory of these struggles is the common heritage of us all. As, with emotions of reverent patriotism, you shall assemble around yonder shaft to-morrow, you will find its foundations deep enough and its proportions large enough to make it a fit monument of the nation's glory.

As heirs of a common inheritance we meet and rejoice together to-night, and as brethren we will celebrate to-morrow. Massachusetts of 1875 is the Massachusetts of 1775. To our guests from the North and from the South, from the East and from the West, we say, "As our fathers greeted your fathers of old, so we now greet you."

Under the ample folds of the old flag we meet as brethren; and as we are stepping upon the threshold of our second century, let us determine that we will make its achievements in all the fields of civilization and peace worthy of a people whose birthright is freedom, whose policy is justice, and "whose God is the Lord."

Under the influence of our glorious old memories, in the midst of the scenes where American liberty in its infancy was rocked, let us declare there shall be no more sectional strife. Let us declare there shall be no warfare, except such as a nation's safety and a nation's honor shall demand, and in that warfare let us all fight together, sympathizing with each other in every danger, and exulting together in every victory.

At the close of the Governor's speech, Major Dexter H. Follett and staff, of the First Battalion of Light Artillery, M. V. M., entered the hall with General Fitz Hugh Lee and the officers of the Norfolk Light Artillery Blues. They were received with immense applause, and escorted to seats on the platform.

The Mayor then said he had been informed that Colonel ANDREWS, of Charleston, South Carolina, was in the hall. The announcement was received with great enthusiasm, and when the Colonel came forward he was heartily cheered.

REMARKS OF COLONEL A. O. ANDREWS.

Fellow-Citizens of Massachusetts: — South Carolina receives with the deepest emotion the greetings of Massachusetts, — an emotion whose tenderness, whose intensity, whose amplitude, can only be measured as when twin sister meets twin sister, and the fiery tribulations, the estranging vicissitudes of the past, are put aside, all lost sight of, all forgotten, in the happy auguries of an unclouded and an undivided future.

How opportune is the happening of these centennials! Verily there is a Providence that shapes our ends. Long, and rugged, and dark, may be the road, but in the fulness of His own good time He causeth light to shine, and in ways unthought by human ken brings about results that fill us with admiring wonder and surprise. Who can fail to be impressed, that, just at this especial juncture, we should be catching sight of, and coming up to, these hundred-mile stones in the journey of our common country, — at the very moment in our history when their sight and presence seem so seasonable, so fortunate, so auspicious, so needed to admonish and to instruct, as well as to cheer and stimulate? First came Lexington and Concord. Old Mecklenburg followed, and in the echoes which yet linger around us we hear the music sounding again with all its primal fervidness and fire, struck from that old chord, as it first broke forth in notes of quickening fraternity, answering to

> "Where once the embattled farmers stood
> And fired the shot heard round the world."

To-day we gather in pious homage around our own consecrated shrine, and join with you in doing reverence where Warren's blood was shed, and renew with you, in family pledge, the sacramental oath, that it shall not have been shed in vain.

Whose heart shall not be lifted into a purer and a sweeter atmosphere, as he hears the tread, and feels the approach, of this grand procession of the mighty past? No dim and shadowy remembrance enclouds them; but they come, all corruscated with light. Like towering cliffs, sublimely they lift their hoary heads. Shooting out amid the rapid current upon which we are surging, they turn our course. In reverential arrest, we pause and ponder. On their scarred fronts we read, furrowed in blood, "truths that wake, to perish never." In our inmost soul, we feel how full of blessing is their presence; how teemingly fruitful, if we but will it so, for a mightier, a far exceeding, a more glorious and beneficently harmonious future! How fraternizing, how hallowing is their influence!

> "Oh, hushed be every thought that springs
> From out the bitterness of things."

Lowly we bend, and ask a blessing and a benison, ere yet we hurry on in the voyage before us.

It is in such a spirit we meet you to-day. Like the worn and jostled members of some large family at Christmas-tide, who have almost unlearned the season as one of merriment, a note of welcome comes for us from the old loved homestead. How the old tie tugs at our heart! Our ears catch the gleeful chimes. Soon bursts out the once familiar carol, —

> "Behold, I bring you good tidings of great joy."

Is this for us? Can we be included? The dear old chant rings out again — and all our misgivings melt away as in jubilant strain is wafted to heaven, "Glory to God in the highest, and on earth peace, good-will to men." Yes, we come! True, in our hands we bring no precious vase, in whose rich loam flowers the costly exotic. We come in homely garb, and with broken cup;

but in that cup is a soil which yonder column will recognize — it is from old Moultrie's sand-bank. You shall plant therein the olive-branch. Old Bunker Hill will catch the gracious dews as they fall from heaven, and gently drop them to nourish its growth, and under its stately shaft it shall find shelter from the scorching sun.

Yes, this is the temper in which we meet you to-day — even as in olden Christmas-tide — and we will closely gather around your honored Yule log, and, as its fragrant smoke curls up, tell o'er with you, in garrulous gossip, of the grand old days a hundred years ago, when in bloody sweat and travail of soul were laid the foundations of this goodly heritage, — alike for us and for you, for South as for North, for West as for East, — from whose lofty towers shall be forever flung its standard of love waving in the breezes of heaven, and inscribed, so that all afar off may read, "Come unto me all ye that labor and are-heavy laden, and I will give you rest." And, oh, see, from our sculptured urns, with what pleased yet anxious serenity look down upon us Warren and Prescott, and Quincy and Hancock, and Otis and Adams, and, interlocking their arms, Gadsden and Moultrie, and Marion and Rutledge and Sumter! And there comes William Washington! How his face glows with its old fire, as he catches sight of, and points Howard and Morgan to his cherished oriflamme, —

"Which at Eutaw shone so bright,
And as a dazzling meteor swept
Through the Cowpens' deadly fight."

Old Bunker Hill grasps it in his arms, and by the memory of their ancient love, by the recollection of their blood-wrought struggles, by the tender recall of the triumphing cheer which is so often wafted from the swamps and fastnesses of the South, he kisses it with fervor true as ancient knight, and, in clarion tones, rings out his tribute to the inspiring guerdon of "a woman withal — but a woman whom Brutus took to wife, and daughter to Cato!"

And now, my friends, when this hallowed jubilation is o'er, and we go back to our homes, what message shall we carry to our reverenced old mother? Never were her sons prouder of her. Never clung they with more filial closeness to her than now in the day of her adversity. Corruption has harried her — misrule has revelled over her; but there she stands, patient and undaunted, in all her matronly purity; never more worthy of our love than as, unruffled amid her assailants, she gathers up the courtly folds of her robe in majestic self-rectitude, her stately eye beaming with the fires of an unstained birthright, and casting to the dust, by its transfigured light, the approaches of insult and dishonor. To her ear the national harp has oft been made to sound "like sweet bells jangled out of tune and harsh." But there is a chord in that harp, a golden chord, which still vibrates in her heart, "musical as Apollo's lute," charming as the harp of Orpheus. It is the chord of these ancient memories; it is the string in that harp, which runs from Moultrie to Bunker Hill. It is the key which, struck at Concord and Lexington, vibrates to Eutaw and King's Mountain. Shall we tell her that you have struck that chord, and that you have struck it with the note, and the music, and the trueness of its ancient song? If so, then indeed shall this day's celebration cause Bunker Hill to be treasured up as the shadow of a great rock, bringing rest, and refreshment, and hope, to pilgrims worn, and heavy, and weary. Then shall we

> "Press heavily onward; not in vain
> Your generous trust in human kind;
> The good which bloodshed could not gain
> Your peaceful zeal shall find."

General FITZ HUGH LEE, of Virginia, was then presented and greeted with enthusiastic cheers by the men, and the waving of handkerchiefs by the ladies. When the excitement had somewhat subsided, he spoke as follows: —

REMARKS OF GENERAL FITZ HUGH LEE.

Mr. Mayor and Ladies and Gentlemen: — I thank you for this most cordial welcome you have extended to my comrades and myself. I came here with the Norfolk Light Artillery Blues, a Confederate organization, whose guns have roared upon many a hard-fought field. As we arrived before your city this afternoon, and were steaming up your beautiful harbor, the first notes that reached me from the band of music sent to meet us were of that good old tune called "Auld Lang Syne;" and I felt I was not going to Boston, but that I was returning again to a common country and a common heritage. I should have wished that my poor presence would have passed unnoticed, and that I might have been permitted to have remained a silent visitor in Boston.

When I remember that this is the first time I have ever stepped on the soil of Massachusetts, I necessarily feel some embarrassment at addressing such a splendid audience as is before me; but when I reflect that I am an American citizen — that I, too, am a descendant of those men who fought on Bunker Hill — I feel that I, too, have a right to be here to celebrate their splendid deeds.

We come here, fellow-citizens, to show that we appreciate the achievements of those patriotic forefathers of ours, — those men who planted the seeds from which our nation sprung. We are here to show by our actual presence that we are fully in sympathy with the sentiment which found expression upon the recent Decoration Days, when loving hands entwined beautiful flowers about the graves of the soldiers of both armies without distinction.

I recall that, right here in Boston, one hundred years ago, a patriotic divine spoke in substance as follows: " We pray thee, O Lord, if our enemies are desirous to fight us, to give them fighting enough; and if there are more on their way across the sea, we pray thee, O Lord, to sink them to the bottom of it." Now, when I see this magnificent demonstration, when my eyes look on yours, beaming with friendliness and heartfelt good-will toward me and mine, I feel that hereafter, if foreign or domestic foes threaten our common country, Massachusetts and Virginia, California and Florida, would shout with one voice, "If they desire to fight, let them have enough."

I may be pardoned if I recall to your minds that in those days of darkness, when the clouds of war enveloped your Commonwealth, my State of Virginia sent right here into your midst him who, in the language of my grandfather, was "first in peace, first in war, and first in the hearts of his countrymen;" he, in the language of Andrew Jackson, "whose character cannot be too profoundly studied and his example too closely followed." Washington appeared here in your midst, brought order out of confusion, and saved our country. I thank you, ladies and gentlemen, most cordially for the manner in which you have received me.

General JUDSON C. KILPATRICK was next introduced, and cordially received.

REMARKS OF GEN. J. C. KILPATRICK.

Fellow-Citizens: — I am proud and happy to assemble with you here to-night on an occasion so important, not only to the people of Massachusetts, but of the whole nation, — an occasion involving elements so sublime, elements which inspire feelings of patriotism worthy of Greece in her best days. It was not my intention to say a word to-night. I entered here but a few moments ago, and had the pleasure of hearing Fitz Hugh Lee, of Virginia, a Confederate soldier, who was my cavalry instructor at West Point, and whom I met on many a bloody battle-field in the late war of the rebellion. And I rejoice, fellow-citizens, to have him come here to-night, and in the presence of this magnificent audience shake hands once again with us beneath the same old Union flag, which is his banner as well as ours. I recognize the fact that it is ten long years since the last hostile shot was fired and since the war-clouds rolled away.

[At this point General SHERMAN appeared upon the platform, and was loudly cheered.]

It will not be becoming in me to continue in the presence of one so well known to this great nation, and whom you would much rather hear speak. [Cries of "Go on. We'll hear him next."] I was about saying that ten long years have passed and gone since the last hostile shot was fired. Monuments of stone rear aloft their heads to heaven to-day from almost every northern village, telling of the patriotic deeds of the brave men who fought in freedom's cause. Little green mounds scattered all over the sunny South are watered alone by women's tears, and women on bended knees are praying over the ruins of what were once palatial homes, and weeping burning tears for dear ones who will return no more. And yet, I know there are men in this country who say "It served them right;" but if they would follow over the wasted stretch of Sherman's march they would find that the beautiful sun shines there, that grain may grow, and that green grass and flowers forever bloom above the spots where brothers beneath opposing banners struggled for the mastery. Let us shake hands here to-night on this happy centennial of the battle of Bunker Hill. Let us unite the North and South, and resolve that the same old flag, henceforth and forever, before us or around us, shall be the pride of our triumph and the shroud of our burial.

REMARKS OF GENERAL WILLIAM T. SHERMAN.

General SHERMAN was then presented. He said:—

I came here to-night to attend a levee of the Mayor of the city of Boston, with no intention of speaking one word; and I hope you will pardon me if I merely express myself somewhat amazed to find myself upon the platform here to-night in the presence of so many gentlemen of Boston, every one of whom can make a better speech than I can. To-morrow you will hear General Devens make a great speech, worthy the occasion, and I want to hear it very much,— so much that I have come fifteen hundred miles to hear it. I want also to stand where Bunker Hill once stood. It is all graded down now ; but the memory of the spot will last long after all of us have disappeared from this earth. Brave deeds, noble actions, there made the beginning of our nation. The deeds done that day, the thoughts thought that day, the courage manifested that day, should make that spot as pure and holy as any spot that can inspire a race. I therefore simply ask you, gentlemen, whose faces are turned toward me to-night, to think of the men who died that day. What has been the result? A nation was born that is influencing the world, and we are come thousands of miles to celebrate its birthday, — one hundred years ago. May you all be better for it, and purer for it, and truer for it, and kinder to each other.

REMARKS OF GENERAL A. E. BURNSIDE.

General BURNSIDE was next introduced by the Mayor. He said : —

I came here to-night as a spectator, and I am not in the least prepared to address such an audience as this. I am a clumsy speaker at best, and it is not proper that I should attempt, on the spur of the moment, to say anything to an assemblage like this. The occasion is one of great importance, and every patriotic heart in the country should be impressed with it. It is my hope and prayer that these centennial days may be so observed as to blot out all feelings of envy or malice which were engendered by the late war. I am free to say here to-night that I am ready to do everything on the face of the earth to accomplish this; I will do anything but acknowledge we were wrong in what we did to suppress the rebellion.

REMARKS OF VICE-PRESIDENT WILSON.

At the close of General Burnside's address there were calls for the Honorable HENRY WILSON, Vice-President of the United States. Yielding reluctantly to the demand made upon him, Mr. WILSON said : —

I respond to your call only for a moment, and I respond for the reason that I cannot say no. We have listened to-night, while we have been welcomed by the Mayor of the city of Boston, who has spoken the words of the whole city. This vast audience has been welcomed here to-night — men from all sections of our country — by the Governor of the State of Massachusetts, and I believe he has spoken the words of all the people of this good old Commonwealth. We have heard a response from South Carolina, and we have welcomed it. We have heard a voice from Old Virginia, and we have welcomed and applauded it. Here, to-night, as a citizen of this Commonwealth, I welcome these men, from all sections of the country, to Massachusetts; and I trust, with God's blessing, this occasion will be consecrated to patriotism, to manhood, to full and impartial liberty to all men of every kindred and race.

I trust that we shall begin the coming century of our country with an acceptance of the sublime doctrine of human right that one hundred years ago animated the men who bared their breasts on Bunker Hill. I believe I have seen already in the South, in the West, in the central States, that this anniversary festival of ours, calling us back to our early history and the grand achievements of our fathers, is accomplishing more for our country than anything that is happening. It is bringing and cementing together the hearts of our people, and Christian men on bended knees should pray for it, patriotic men should labor for it, and we should know that we live in a country that is to be our country; that we live in a country where men of all races are brothers. I believe, gentlemen, that we should all strive for harmony, unity, justice, for equal rights to everybody in our land.

This closed the formal part of the exercises, and introductions and conversation followed.

THE PROCESSION.

TRIUMPHAL ARCH. ENTRANCE TO CITY HALL SQUARE, CHARLESTOWN.
[Drawn by EDWIN A. ABBEY. Engraved by W. J. LINTON.]

THE PROCESSION.

The General Court having made the Seventeenth of June, 1875, a legal public holiday, the public buildings and offices throughout the State were closed, and all business, except that connected with the celebration, was suspended. At an early hour in the morning the various organizations which were to take part in the proceedings of the day began to arrive in the city and take position in the places assigned to them. The streets were thronged by people from all parts of the country, who were desirous of witnessing what promised to be the most extensive and magnificent military and civic display ever made in New England.

The favorable state of the weather added greatly to the success of the occasion; a mild east wind prevailed throughout the day, and tempered the heat so that those who marched in the procession, and those who stood long hours in the streets to see it pass, were enabled to do so without discomfort.

All the public buildings and many private dwellings and places of business, especially those along the route of the procession, were handsomely decorated with flags, bunting and flowers. At all points of historic interest connected with the battle of Bunker Hill, or with the revolutionary period, inscriptions were placed, giving a clear and concise statement of the event to be commemorated.

Across the northerly end of Charles-river avenue, where the procession entered City square, Charlestown, a triumphal arch was erected. One of the pillars bore a representation of the battle of Bunker Hill, with the date "1775" beneath; on the other was a view of the present Monument, and the date "1875." On the keystone of the arch was inscribed

"HEROES OF BUNKER HILL,"

and on either side were the names of PRESCOTT, PUTNAM, WARREN, KNOWLTON, STARK, and POMEROY, — the one first mentioned occupying the highest place of honor.

At nine o'clock in the morning the members of the City Government, the guests of the city, and the persons invited by His Honor the Mayor to join the procession, assembled at the City Hall, and proceeded thence, by invitation of His Excellency the Governor, to the State House, to witness the military review.

At ten o'clock the troops moved from their rendezvous on the Common, passing out at the corner of Charles street and Boylston street, and marched through Boylston, Tremont and Beacon streets, past the reviewing party, which occupied a platform in front of the State House.

The movement of the procession was somewhat delayed by the review, and it was not until a quarter past one o'clock that the Chief Marshal was enabled to enter upon the line of march. The formation was as follows: —

The Chief of Police, with fifteen mounted men.
The Fall River Brass Band.
The Fourth Battalion of Infantry M. V. M., Major Austin C. Wellington commanding.
General FRANCIS A. OSBORN, Chief Marshal.
The Members of his Staff, namely: —
Col. W. V. Hutchings, Chief of Staff.
Col. Cornelius G. Attwood, Adjutant General.
Col. Solomon Hovey, Jr., Assistant Adjutant General.

Capt. James Thompson, Chief Quartermaster.
Lieut. Edward B. Richardson, Chief Signal Officer.

Mr. James Swords,	Mr. M. F. Dickinson, Jr.,
Capt. Nathan Appleton,	Mr. B. F. Hatch,
Capt. Geo. P. Denny,	Mr. Howard L. Porter,
Mr. W. A. Tower,	Capt. Geo. A. Fisher,
Gen. W. W. Blackmar,	Mr. Wendell Goodwin,
Col. W. H. Long,	Capt. John Read,
Col. Chas. H. Hooper,	Mr. A. W. Hobart,
Mr. Jas. Lawrence.	Major William P. Shreve,
Mr. A. G. Hodges,	Capt. A. E. Proctor,
Col. Nathaniel Wales,	Lieut. H. G. O. Colby,
Mr. Samuel Tuckerman,	Capt. Edward F. Devens,
Capt. G. A. Churchill,	Mr. H. G. Parker,
Mr. Arthur L. Devens,	Capt. Chas. A. Campbell,
Capt. W. A. Couthouy,	Mr. John B. Draper,
Mr. M. S. P. Williams,	Mr. C. G. Pease,
Col. Geo. C. Joslin,	Lieut. Augustus N. Sampson,
Mr. Otis Kimball, Jr.,	Mr. James G. Freeman,
Col. Louis N. Tucker,	Mr. E. P. Kennard,
Col. John C. Whiton,	Mr. F. W. Lincoln, Jr.,
Mr. M. A. Aldrich,	Mr. G. Henry Williams,
Mr. J. R. Wolston,	Capt. John H. Alley.
Mr. Wm. M. Paul,	

Signal Corps.

MASSACHUSETTS VOLUNTEER MILITIA.

Brown's Brigade Band.

The First Corps of Cadets M. V. M., Lieutenant Colonel Thomas F. Edmands commanding.

His Excellency WILLIAM GASTON, Governor and Commander-in-Chief.

The Members of his Staff, namely: —

Major Gen. James A. Cunningham, Adjutant General.
Col. Isaac F. Kingsbury, Assistant Adjutant General.
Col. Albert A. Haggett, Assistant Inspector General.

Brig. Gen. P. A. Collins, Judge Advocate General.
Col. Charles W. Wilder, Assistant Quartermaster General.
Brig. Gen. William J. Dale, Surgeon General.
Col. Joshua B. Treadwell, Assistant Surgeon General.
Col. Edward Lyman, Col. James A. Rumrill, Col. Leverett S. Tuckerman, Col. Edward Gray, Aids to Commander-in-Chief.
Col. George H. Campbell, Military Secretary.
The Salem Brass Band.
The Second Corps of Cadets M. V. M., Lieutenant Colonel A. Parker Browne commanding.
Major General Benjamin F. Butler, commanding Division Massachusetts Militia.
The Members of his Staff, namely: —
Col. Edgar J. Sherman, Assistant Adjutant General.
Col. Yorick G. Hurd, Medical Director.
Lieut. Col. Edward J. Jones, Assistant Inspector General.
Lieut. Col. George J. Carney, Assistant Quartermaster.
Major John W. Kimball, Engineer.
Major Roland G. Usher, Aide-de-camp.
Major Edwin L. Barney, Judge Advocate.
THE SECOND BRIGADE M. V. M., Brigadier General George H. Peirson commanding.
The Lynn Brass Band.
The Eighth Regiment of Infantry, Colonel Benjamin F. Peach, Jr., commanding.
The Sixth Regiment of Infantry, Colonel Melvin Beal commanding.
The Fifth Regiment Band.
The Fifth Regiment of Infantry, Colonel Ezra J. Trull commanding.
The Lawrence Brass Band.
The Second Battalion of Light Artillery, Major George S. Merrill commanding.
The Dunstable Cornet Band.
Company F, Unattached Cavalry, Chelmsford, Captain Christopher Roby commanding.
THE FIRST BRIGADE M. V. M., Brigadier General Isaac S. Burrell commanding.

The Ninth Regiment Band.
The Ninth Regiment of Infantry, Colonel Bernard F. Finan commanding.
The First Regiment Band.
The First Regiment of Infantry, Colonel Henry W. Wilson commanding.
The Third Regiment Band.
The Third Regiment of Infantry, Colonel Bradford D. Davol commanding.
The National Band, Boston.
The Second Battalion of Infantry, Major Lewis Gaul commanding.
The Woonsocket Brass Band.
The First Battalion of Light Artillery, Captain Charles W. Baxter commanding.
The Chelsea Brass Band.
The First Battalion of Cavalry, Lieutenant Colonel John H. Roberts commanding.
THE THIRD BRIGADE M. V. M., Brigadier General Robert H. Chamberlain commanding.
The Hartford City Band.
The Second Regiment of Infantry, Colonel Joseph B. Parsons commanding.
Richardson's Band, Worcester.
The Tenth Regiment of Infantry, Colonel James M. Drennan commanding.
The Worcester National Band.
The Fifth Battery of Light Artillery, Captain John G. Rice commanding.

FIRST DIVISION.

Major Henry L. Higginson, Chief of Division.

Aids: Captain John C. Jones, Assistant Adjutant General; Mr. Henry Upham, Mr. Wm. B. Bacon, Jr., Mr. A. C. Tower, Mr. Daniel C. Bacon, Mr. Frank Seabury.

This division was composed of military organizations from other States, namely:—

The Seventh Regiment Band and Drum Corps, New York.
The Seventh Regiment National Guard, State of New York, Colonel Emmons Clark commanding.
The First Regiment Band, Pennsylvania.
The First Regiment National Guard of Pennsylvania, Colonel R. Dale Benson commanding.
The Second Regiment Band, Pennsylvania.
The Second Regiment National Guard of Pennsylvania, Lieutenant Colonel Harmanius Neff commanding.
Ringold's Band, Reading, Pa.
The State Fencibles, Philadelphia, Pa., Captain John W. Ryan commanding.
McClurg's Cornet Band, Philadelphia.
The Washington Grays, of Philadelphia, Captain Louis D. Baugh commanding.
The Independence Band, Wilmington, Del.
The Philadelphia Gray Invincibles, Captain A. Oscar Jones commanding.
The American Brass Band, Providence, R. I.
The First Rhode Island Light Infantry Regiment, Colonel R. H. I. Goddard commanding.
The National Band, Providence, R. I.
The Meagher Guards, Providence, R. I., Captain Peter McHugh commanding.
Colt's Armory Band, Hartford, Conn.
The Hillyer Guards, Hartford, Conn., Captain John T. Sherman commanding.
Repetti's Band, Washington, D. C.
The Washington Light Infantry, Washington, D. C., Captain William G. Moore commanding.
The Governor Straw Rifles, Manchester, N. H., Colonel John J. Dillon commanding.
The Mansfield Guard, Middletown, Conn., Captain R. Graham commanding.

The Marine Band, U. S. N., Washington, D. C.
The Fifth Maryland Regiment, Colonel J. Stricker Jenkins commanding.

SECOND DIVISION.

Colonel Henry R. Sibley, Chief of Division.

Aids: Captain George R. Kelso, Assistant Adjutant General; Mr. Retire H. Parker, Mr. John H. Dee, Mr. George T. Childs, Mr. Edwin F. Peirce.

This division included the City Government of Boston, the Guests of the City, the State Government of Massachusetts, and the Guests of the State, in carriages. The formation was as follows:—

Edmands' Military Band, with Drum Corps.
Companies D and E, Fifth Artillery, U. S. A., Brevet Major General Richard Arnold, U. S. A., commanding.

CITY GOVERNMENT AND GUESTS.

His Honor Samuel C. Cobb, Mayor of Boston; and His Honor William H. Wickham, Mayor of New York.
General Fitz John Porter, Commissioner of Public Works, New York; Colonel E. L. Gaul, Secretary to the Mayor of New York; Nelson H. Tappan, the Comptroller of New York.
Aldermen John T. Clark and Thomas B. Harris; His Honor R. L. Fulton, Mayor of Galveston, Texas; and Colonel Etting, representing His Honor William S. Stokely, Mayor of Philadelphia.
Aldermen S. B. Stebbins and S. M. Quincy; His Honor Peter Jones, Mayor of Jacksonville, Fla.; and His Honor Joshua L. Simons, Mayor of Wilmington, Del.
Alderman James Power, and Halsey J. Boardman, Esq., President of the Common Council; His Honor W. P. Connerlay, Mayor of Wilmington, N. C.; and His Honor R. M. Richardson, Mayor of Portland, Me.
Councilmen Edwin Sibley and Isaac P. Clarke; His Honor Henry G. Lewis, Mayor of New Haven, Conn.; and His Honor Alpheus Gay, Mayor of Manchester, N. H.

Councilmen Francis H. Peabody and John N. Devereux; Alderman Mackey of Charleston, S. C.; and Hon. William Bigler of Philadelphia, Financial Agent Centennial Commission.

Councilmen Eugene H. Sampson and Curtis Guild; General Joseph R. Hawley, President of the U. S. Centennial Commission; and Alfred T. Goshorn, Esq., Director General U. S. Centennial Commission.

Hon. Daniel J. Morrell, Chairman Executive Committee U. S. Centennial Commission; Dr. Buckminster Brown, husband of the grand-daughter of General Joseph Warren; Warren Putnam Newcomb, great-great-grandson of General Warren and General Putnam; and Dr. Edward Warren.

His Honor Henry L. Williams, Mayor of Salem; His Honor Isaac Bradford, Mayor of Cambridge; His Honor Abraham H. Howland, Mayor of New Bedford; and His Honor Jacob M. Lewis, Mayor of Lynn.

His Honor D. F. Atkinson, Mayor of Newburyport; His Honor R. H. Tewksbury, Mayor of Lawrence; His Honor James F. Davenport, Mayor of Fall River; and His Honor Charles H. Ferson, Mayor of Chelsea.

His Honor George H. Babbitt, Mayor of Taunton; His Honor Wm. H. Furber, Mayor of Somerville; His Honor W. B. Pearsons, Mayor of Holyoke; and His Honor Robert R. Fears, Mayor of Gloucester.

His Honor James F. C. Hyde, Mayor of Newton; Hon. Charles Francis Adams; and Hon. William Gray.

Mr. Ralph Waldo Emerson, Hon. Ebenezer Rockwood Hoar, Mr. Joseph Heywood, of Concord, and Hon. Otis Norcross.

Mr. W. H. Munroe, of Lexington; Hon. Josiah Quincy, Hon. Alexander H. Rice, and Hon. Joseph M. Wightman.

Dr. J. V. C. Smith, Mr. John Cummings, of Woburn; Hon. J. J. Clarke, and Hon. Linus B. Comins.

Hon. Geo. Lewis, Hon. S. S. Sleeper, Mr. Joseph W. Tucker, and Hon. E. L. Norton.

Hon. Liverus Hull, Hon. P. J. Stone, Hon. Jas. Adams, and His Honor Alpheus Currier, Mayor of Haverhill.

Members of the City Council of Boston (not included in the Committee of Arrangements), and heads of City Departments.
The American Band of Cambridge.
The National Lancers, Captain Cyrus C. Emery commanding.

THE STATE GOVERNMENT AND GUESTS.

Hon. Henry Wilson, the Vice-President of the United States; Hon. George B. Loring, President of the Massachusetts Senate; Mr. Justice Strong, of the United States Supreme Court;
and Rev. W. E. Strong, of Roxbury.
Hon. Willard P. Phillips, of Salem; Mr. Samuel May, of Leicester; His Excellency Stephen Preston, the Haytien Minister; and
His Excellency Señor Don Francisco Gonzales Errazuriz, the Chilian Minister.
General William T. Sherman, Major General Irwin McDowell, Col. J. C. Audenried, of Gen. Sherman's staff; and
Hon. E. D. Winslow.
Bvt. Major General Nelson A. Miles, 5th Infantry U. S. A.; Bvt. Brigadier General O. M. Poe, U. S. A.; Bvt. Brigadier General J. E. Tourtellotte, of General Sherman's staff;
and Bvt. Major General E. W. Hinks.
General T. J. Haines, Col. Theodore T. S. Laidley, Captain W. R. Livermore, and C. E. Jewett.
Hon. Hannibal Hamlin, United States Senator from Maine; Hon. Thomas W. Ferry, United States Senator from Michigan;
Hon. George S. Boutwell, United States Senator from Massachusetts; and Mr. Enoch H.
Towne, of Worcester.
Gen. Thomas Kilby Smith, of Gen. Sherman's staff; Hon. C. P. Thompson, Hon. B. W. Harris, and Hon. Rufus S. Frost, Representatives in Congress from Massachusetts.
Hon. Eugene Hale, and Hon. John H. Burleigh, Representatives in Congress from Maine; Hon. John K. Tarbox, Representative in Congress from Massachusetts; and
Judge Waldo Colburn.
Chandler's Band, of Portland.
The Portland Cadets, Captain N. D. Winslow commanding,
escorting

His Excellency Nelson Dingley, Jr., Governor of Maine, and staff; Speaker Thomas, of the Maine House of Representatives, and Hon. Francis D. Stedman, of the Massachusetts Senate.

His Excellency Person C. Cheney, Governor of New Hampshire, and staff.

Drum Corps.

First Company Governor's Foot Guard of Hartford, Major John C. Parsons commanding,

escorting

His Excellency Charles R. Ingersoll, Governor of Connecticut, and staff; General Walter Harriman, U. S. Naval Officer, and General A. B. Underwood, U. S. Surveyor, of Boston.

His Excellency Henry S. Lippitt, Governor of Rhode Island, and staff.

His Excellency Joseph D. Bedle, Governor of New Jersey, and staff; and Hon. T. J. Dacey, of the Massachusetts Senate.

The first troop of City Cavalry, Philadelphia,

escorting

His Excellency John F. Hartranft, Governor of Pennsylvania, and staff, mounted.

His Excellency Adelbert Ames, Governor of Mississippi; His Excellency J. D. Bagley, Governor of Michigan; Hon. George F. Shepley, Judge of the United States Circuit Court; and Hon. George P. Sanger, U. S. District Attorney.

Mr. Chief Justice Gray and Associate Justices Wells, Endicott and Ames, of the Supreme Judicial Court of Massachusetts.

Col. George L. Browne, of the Old Guard, State Fencibles of Philadelphia; ex-Gov. Emory Washburn; Hon. Wm. A. Simmons, Collector of the port of Boston.

Lieut.-Gov. Horatio G. Knight, and Hon. Geo. Whitney, Hon. Seth Turner and Hon. Geo. O. Brastow, of the Executive Council.

Hon. E. H. Brewster, Hon. Alden Leland, Hon. J. K. Baker and Hon. E. H. Dunn, of the Executive Council.

Hon. R. Couch; Senator Wm. H. Phillips of Berkshire; and Senator Geo. A. Davis, of Essex.

Hon. Oliver Warner, Secretary of State; Hon. Charles Adams, Jr., Treasurer and Receiver-General; Hon. Charles Endicott, Auditor; and Hon. Charles R. Train, Attorney-General.

Mr. Charles Hale of the House; Ensign H. Kellogg, Charles A. Phelps, ex-Speakers of the House of Representatives; and Col. Joseph A. Harwood, of the Senate.

The members of the Senate and House of Representatives of the General Court of Massachusetts.

THIRD DIVISION.

Colonel Charles E. Fuller, Chief of Division.

AIDS.

Col. F. R. Appleton, Assistant Adjutant General; Col. S. D. Warren, Jr., Col. J. H. Welles, Capt. Roswell C. Downer, Lieut. Henry E. Warner, Col. J. L. Baker.

This division was composed of the following organizations:—

The Massachusetts Commandery of the Military Order of the Loyal Legion of the United States, under command of Gen. Francis W. Palfrey, accompanied by Major General A. E. Burnside. [On the top of the staff which bore their banner was perched a solid silver eagle, which was presented to the New England Guards, by Arnold Wells, in 1812. It was carried by the Guards at the laying of the corner-stone of Bunker Hill Monument, 1825, and again at the completion of the Monument, 1843.]

The Bunker Hill Monument Association, in carriages; President George Washington Warren; with Hon. Charles Devens, Jr., the orator of the day.

The Officers of the Grand Lodge of Masons in Massachusetts, Percival L. Everett, Grand Master. [The Grand Master wore the apron which belonged to General Joseph Warren at the time of his death. Dr. Winslow Lewis, Deputy Grand Master, wore the apron once belonging to Gen. Lafayette, and which was worn at the laying of the corner-stone of Bunker Hill Monument.]

The carriage formerly belonging to Governor Eustis, and in which Lafayette was accustomed to ride when he was his guest, occupied by Mr. William E. Baker, the present owner, and by Hon. Marshall P. Wilder, President of the New England Historic-Genealogical Society.

The New England Historic-Genealogical Society, in carriages. Delegates: Hon. Israel Washburn, Jr., Maine; W. B. Towne, Esq., New Hampshire; Hon. William Hill, Vermont; Hon. John I. Bartlett, Rhode Island.

The American Antiquarian Society of Worcester, in a carriage. Delegates: S. F. Haven, Esq., Dr. Joseph Sargent, Dr. Rufus Woodward, Dr. Nathaniel Paine.

Pilgrim Association of Plymouth. Delegates: W. T. Davis, President; I. N. Stoddard, W. S. Danforth, E. C. Sherman, W. H. Whitman.

The Massachusetts Society of the Order of the Cincinnati. Forty delegates in carriages, under President Admiral H. K. Thatcher.

Eliot Band of Boston.

The Massachusetts Charitable Mechanics' Association, President Nathaniel Adams.

Massachusetts Veterans of 1812. Association represented by Major Nathan Warren.

The Boston Charitable Irish Society, Bernard Corr, President.

FOURTH DIVISION.

Col. Thos. L. Livermore, Chief of Division.

AIDS.

Col. Charles E. Hapgood, Assistant Adjutant General; Col. Thomas E. Barker, Col. Daniel K. Cross, Major Benj. F. Weeks, Major Geo. E. Fayerweather.

This division was composed of veteran organizations formed into a Brigade, under the command of Major Dexter H. Follett, as follows:—

The Germania Band of Boston.
The Ancient and Honorable Artillery Company, organized in 1638, Major General Nathaniel P. Banks commanding.
The Redwood Band of Newport, R. I.
The Newport (R. I.) Artillery Veteran Association, organized in 1741, Colonel Julius Sayer commanding, accompanied by officers of the Newport Artillery Company.
The United States Naval Band of Portsmouth, N. H.
The Newburyport, Mass., Veteran Artillery Company, organized in 1775, Col. E. E. Stone commanding.
The Saunders Band of Peabody, Mass.
The Salem (Mass.) Light Infantry Veteran Association, organized in 1805, Col. John F. Fellows commanding.
The Veteran Association Band of Providence.
The First Light Infantry Veteran Association of Providence, R. I., organized in 1818, Major-General W. W. Brown commanding.
The Veteran Seventh Regiment Band, New York.
The Veteran National Guard, 7th Regiment, State of New York, Colonel Marshall Lefferts commanding.
The Manchester (N. H.) Cornet Band.
The Amoskeag Veterans, of Manchester, N. H., Major George C. Gilmore commanding.
The Putnam Phalanx Drum Corps.
The Putnam Phalanx, of Hartford, Connecticut, Major Henry Kennedy commanding.

Downing's Ninth Regiment Band, of New York.

The Old Guard, of New York, Major G. W. McLean commanding,
Accompanied by

Bvt. Brigadier General Washington Hadley, J. T. Howe, Esq., Major J. W. Hazlet, and C. D. Fredericks, Esq.

The Washington Light Infantry, of Charleston, S. C., Major R. C. Gilchrist, First Lieutenant, commanding,
Accompanied by

Col. Thomas Y. Simons, Col. A. O. Andrews, J. Lawrence Honour, Esq.

The Norfolk Light Artillery Blues, of Norfolk, Va., four guns, Captain James W. Gilmer commanding.

Carriages containing, as guests of the Blues, Gen. Fitz Hugh Lee, who commanded a division of Confederate cavalry during the late war; Col. Walter H. Taylor, who was Adjutant General to Gen. Robert E. Lee; Col. Stark, who commanded Norfolk troops; Capt. E. B. White, who was of the Confederate Navy; Mr. M. Glennan of the Norfolk *Virginian;* and C. E. Perkins of the Norfolk *Landmark.*

Drum Corps.

Old Columbians, organized in 1792, Capt. Michael Doherty commanding.

Amesbury Veteran Artillery Association Band.

The Amesbury and Salisbury Veteran Association, Capt. Newell Boyd commanding.

Decorated carriage, containing twelve old sailors, and also a piece of ordnance cast in 1736, and taken from Fort Point channel.

FIFTH DIVISION.

Chief of Division, Gen. J. Cushing Edmands.

AIDS.

Col. Edward B. Blasland, Assistant Adjutant General; Capt. T. R. Matthews, Gen. E. Blakeslee, Lieut. Wm. H. Bird, Lieut. C. M. Haley.

American Band of Boston.
Lexington Minute Men, Acting Major, E. L. Zalinski, U. S. A.
Boston School Regiment Drum Corps.
Boston School Regiment, Colonel William B. Lawrence commanding.
The Latin School Battalion, Major Edward Robinson commanding.
First Battalion English High School, Major E. C. Wilde commanding.
Second Battalion, English High School, Major George Nickerson commanding.
The Highland Battalion, Major A. L. Jacobs commanding.
Drum Corps.
The Cambridge Cadets, of East Cambridge, Capt. E. A. Cooney commanding.
Drum Corps.
The Chelmsford Minute Men, of Chelmsford, Mass.
The Boston Caledonian Club, John Stark, Chief.
The Thorndike Horse Guards, of Beverly, Captain Hugh Hill commanding.
The Magoun Battery, of Medford, Captain Charles Russell commanding.
The Franco-Belgian Benevolent Society, in barouches, with American, French and Belgian colors.
The Boston Highland Benevolent Association, in a barge.

SIXTH DIVISION.

Chief of Division, Charles B. Fox.

AIDS.

Col. Francis S. Hesseltine, Major Cyrus S. Haldeman, Major Frank Goodwin, Lieutenants Henry D. Pope, and Wm. Chickering.
Charles Russell Lowell Post No. 7, G. A. R., of Boston, Thomas M. Kenney, commander.
Berry's Band of Lowell.
Benjamin F. Butler Post No. 42, of Lowell, G. W. Huntoon, commander.

Stoneham Brass Band.

Radiant Star Council No. 5, Order of United American Mechanics of South Boston, Commander Edward Isaacs.

Delegates from Bay State Council No. 1, of Boston; Bunker Hill Council No. 2, of Charlestown; High Rock Council No. 6, of Lynn; Harvard Council No. 9, of Cambridge; Israel Putnam Council No. 10, of Boston; Niagara Council No. 11, of Salem; Warren Council No. 13, of Lynn; Abraham Lincoln Council No. 14, of Somerville; Sagamore Council No. 15, of Saugus; Roxbury Council No. 17, of Boston Highlands; all members of the O. U. A. M. organization.

Delegates from the Junior Order United American Mechanics of Massachusetts.

Representatives of the National and Massachusetts State Councils, O. U. A. M., in barouches.

Bond's Brass Band, of Boston.

Ivanhoe Lodge, Knights of Pythias No. 13, of Charlestown, T. W. Paine, commander.

Delegates from Washington Lodge No. 10, of South Boston; Commonwealth Lodge No. 19, of Boston; King Solomon Lodge No. 18, of Boston; Socrates Lodge No. 21, of South Boston; Old Colony Lodge No. 43, of Abington; Mattapan Lodge No. 44, of Dorchester; all Knights of Pythias.

American Brass Band of Suncook, N. H.

Oriental Lodge, Knights of Pythias, of Suncook, N. H., H. D. Wood, commander.

Johnson's Drum Corps.

Colored Veteran Association, Major Burt Smith commanding.

Delegates from the Colored Veteran Association of Norfolk, Va., accompanied by Inspector General J. Mullen, of the Grand Army Order of Virginia, and North and South Carolina.

SEVENTH DIVISION.

John T. Bamrick, Chief of Division.

AIDS.

Edward Riley, Assistant Adjutant General; Patrick O'Riorden, Dennis Crowley, James H. Lombard, Timothy C. Mahoney, Daniel Heffernan.

This division was composed of Catholic Benevolent Societies, as follows: —

O'Connor's mounted Band.
Knights of St. Patrick, composed of two mounted companies, one from Boston, Capt. Lyons commanding;
Another from Lawrence, Mass., Timothy Dacey commanding.
Company A, of the Legion of St. Patrick, Gen. J. H. Henchon commanding.
The United Association of American Hibernians of South Boston, John McCaffrey, Chief Marshal.
Union Brass Band of Lynn.
St. Joseph Cadets, Captain J. F. Lynch commanding.
St. Joseph Drum Corps.

Ancient Order of Hibernians in several divisions, namely: —

Division No. 1, of Boston, Lawrence Donovan commanding.
Belknap Brass Band, of Quincy.
Division No. 2, of East Boston, John C. McDevitt commanding.
Division No. 3, of Jamaica Plain, D. J. Curley commanding.
Brookline Band.
Division No. 4, of Boston, J. J. Leevens commanding.
Brookline Hibernian Band.
Division No. 5, of Salem, Timothy Foley commanding.
Lynn Cornet Band.
Division No. 8, Jamaica Plain, James McMorrow commanding.
Delegation of the American Society of Hibernians in a barouche.

EIGHTH DIVISION.

John O'Brien, Chief of Division.

AIDS.

Lawrence P. Furlong, Assistant Adjutant General; Patrick Coyle, J. H. O'Neil, A. J. Phillip, L. C. Dugan; Orderly, John Calanan.

Hibernia Brass Band, Natick.

Fulton Cadets, Capt. J. J. Barry commanding.

St. Valentine Cadets, two companies, Major Thomas Kelley commanding.

St. Valentine Total Abstinence Society, Marshal, T. H. Good.

Cathedral Cadets, Captain M. Mahoney commanding.

Drum Corps.

Father Mathew Cadets, Malden, Captain D. J. Murphy commanding.

Loyola Temperance Cadets, Melrose, Captain James C. Campbell commanding.

Highland Drum Corps.

Cathedral Temperance Society, Marshal, J. J. Nolan.

St. Joseph Total Abstinence Society, Marshal, Jeremiah Sheehy.

Father Mathew Drum Corps.

Father Mathew Total Abstinence Society, Lynn, Marshal, Joseph Murphy.

South Boston Division, Total Abstinence Society, Marshal, E. J. Flaherty.

Drum Corps.

Gate of Heaven Cadets, Colonel E. Haynes commanding.

Drum Corps.

St. Vincent's Total Abstinence Society, Marshal, D. Fahey.

Saxonville Brass Band, with Drum Corps.

Saints Peter and Paul Total Abstinence Society, Marshal, William Ward.

Drum Corps.

St. Augustine Total Abstinence Society, Marshal, Michael Creed.

South Boston Young Men's Total Abstinence Society, Marshal, C. J. Ford.

St. James Temperance Drum Corps.
St. James Total Abstinence Society, Marshal, James Cotter.
Drum Corps.
St. James Young Men's Total Abstinence Society, Marshal, L. J. Crowley.
Drum Corps.
Saint Rose Total Abstinence and Benevolent Society, Chelsea, Marshal, Daniel McGivern.
Saint Rose Cadets, Chelsea, Captain Wm. Evans commanding.
St. Stephen Drum Corps.
Saint Stephen "Guard of Honor" Cadets, Major J. H. Flaherty commanding.
Independent Band, East Boston.
St. Stephens Total Abstinence Society, Marshal, John H. Rohen.
East Boston Total Abstinence Society, Marshal, P. J. Flanagan.

NINTH DIVISION.

Levi L. Willcutt, Esq., Chief of Division.

AIDS.

Major Charles B. Whittemore, Assistant Adjutant General; Captain Fred R. Shattuck, Mr. Nelson V. Titus, Mr. Charles F. Curtis, Mr. Francis H. Willcutt, Mr. Benjamin W. Parker, Mr. George L. Damon, Mr. William B. Pearce, Mr. Charles M. Dunlap, Mr. Alfred S. Taylor.

This division was composed of representations from the merchants, mechanics and manufacturers of Boston. Although the proposition to make such a display was not acted upon until a few days before the celebration was to take place, it was then entered into with such enthusiasm as to produce the most gratifying result. The extent and variety of the exhibition has never been equalled in this country. There were two hundred and thirty-three business houses and manufactories represented by four hundred and twenty-one teams, fifteen hundred and eighty-seven harnessed horses, and twelve hundred men. Most of the teams were handsomely decorated, and many of them bore inscriptions of a patriotic or humorous character. The wagons were loaded with the articles sold or produced by the exhibitors, and in some cases with workmen who appeared in the exercise of their vocation.

The finest exhibitions were made by the furniture-dealers, piano and organ manufacturers, glass-blowers, leather-dealers, grocers, brewers, bakers, and florists. The brewers appeared with fifty wagons and one hundred and eight horses; the furniture-dealers with thirty-six wagons and eighty-six horses; the piano and organ manufacturers with twenty-eight wagons and ninety horses — one firm alone having twelve four-horse teams; and the leather-dealers with nineteen wagons and fifty-two horses. The furniture-dealers and the bakers were preceded by bands of music.

This division closed the procession. Throughout the route the sidewalks and fronts of buildings were crowded with spectators. In many places where there were vacant lots, platforms or tiers of seats had been erected and were let at high prices. From an official return obtained from the several steam railway companies whose cars enter the city, it appears that the number of persons brought into the city in that way during the day was one hundred and forty thousand. If we add to this the number of persons who arrived previous to that day, and the number of our own citizens who were called out by the display, it is evident that the procession was witnessed by not less than five hundred thousand people. The chief officers of the City and State, and their distinguished guests, were greeted with cheers and shouts of welcome as they passed along the crowded streets.

The scene on Columbus avenue, as the long column of troops passed up from Dartmouth street, was especially grand and imposing. The houses were all richly decorated with flags, banners, shields, pictures and mottoes. At the head of the avenue, where the procession turned into Chester park, a large ornamented stand had been erected, with seats rising one above another to a great height. The upper seats were occupied entirely by school children, who waved miniature flags as the troops passed along, keeping time in their motions with the music of the bands.

The time occupied by the procession in passing a given point (all delays being deducted) was three hours and fifty minutes.

SERVICES ON BUNKER HILL.

BUNKER HILL.

[Drawn by EDWIN A. ABBEY. Engraved by A. V. S. ANTHONY.]

SERVICES ON BUNKER HILL.

The services on Bunker Hill were held in a large pavilion, erected on the southerly side of the Monument grounds. The civic portion of the procession reached the hill about a quarter before six o'clock, and the seats in the pavilion were soon filled. The platform, which faced the Monument, was occupied by the distinguished guests of the Monument Association, the City, and the State.

At six o'clock Colonel HENRY WALKER, Chief Marshal of the Association, called the company to order, and said: —

Ladies and Gentlemen: — I have the pleasure of introducing to you Hon. George Washington Warren as President of the Bunker Hill Monument Association and as President of the Day.

The announcement was received with applause; and Judge WARREN, advancing to the front of the platform, said: —

Ladies and Gentlemen: — With devout thankfulness for the auspicious manner in which this day has been observed, let us look up to the Supreme Being for His blessing.

Rev. Rufus Ellis, D. D., pastor of the First Church of Boston, then offered the following prayer: —

PRAYER BY REV. RUFUS ELLIS, D. D.

God of all power and grace, as we gather about our pillar of remembrance, let it be into Thy holy presence. We adore the wonder of Thy providence and that faithfulness which is unto all generations. On this day of high and holy memories we praise Thee, the God of our fathers, the hope of their hearts in their day of trial. Thou didst lead them through the cloud and through the sea, and gave unto them their portion amongst the nations; and in all these years Thou hast watched over us, and hast led us safely through our days of darkness, and made us one nation before Thee. As we gather from the East and from the West, from the North and from the South, to the battle-field of our nation, let it be into a fellowship of love and service. Make the word which shall be spoken to us this day Thy word, that every blessed faith, hope and charity may be deepened in our hearts and our land brought nearer to the kingdom of Thy dear Son. Under the heavens which He hath opened, and in the spirit which He hath given, and in the words which He hath taught, let us all say unto Thee, "Our Father, who art in heaven, hallowed be Thy name. Thy kingdom come, Thy will be done on earth as it is done in heaven. Give us this day our daily bread, and forgive us our trespasses as we forgive those who trespass against us; and lead us not into temptation, but deliver us from evil, for Thine is the kingdom, and the power, and the glory, for ever and ever. Amen."

At the conclusion of the prayer, the Apollo Club, under the direction of Mr. B. J. Lang, sang the following hymn, entitled " Prayer Before the Battle."

>Hear us, Almighty One!
>Hear us, all holy One!
>>Lord of the battle before us!
>Father, all praise to Thee,
>Father, all thanks to Thee,
>>That Freedom's banner is o'er us!
>
>Like a consuming brand,
>Stretch forth Thy mighty hand,
>>Wrong and oppression destroying.
>Help us, O Lord of right!
>Help us, O God of might!
>>Help us, where war-tides are flowing.
>
>Help us, though we may fall;
>From out the grave we call;
>>Praise to Thy name, and forever.
>All power and glory be
>Thine through eternity!
>>Help us, Almighty One! Amen.

Judge WARREN then said: It is with extreme pleasure that I have the honor to present to you our esteemed associate, the soldier, the scholar, and the jurist, CHARLES DEVENS, Jr.

GENERAL DEVENS was received with hearty applause. After acknowledging the greeting of the audience he proceeded to deliver the following address : —

ADDRESS OF GENERAL DEVENS.

Fellow-Citizens: — In pious and patriotic commemoration of the great deed which one hundred years ago was done on this immortal field; in deep thankfulness for the blessings which have been showered upon us as a people with so lavish a hand; in the earnest hope that the liberty, guarded and sustained by the sanctions of law, which the valor of our fathers won for us, and which we hold to-day in solemn trust, may be transmitted to endless generations, — we have gathered in this countless throng, representing in its assemblage every portion of our common country.

A welcome, cordial, generous, and heartfelt, to each and all!

Welcome to the sons of New England, and their descendants, no matter where their homes may be! They stand upon the soil made sacred now and forever by the blood of their fathers. Among them we recognize with peculiar pleasure and satisfaction those allied by family ties to the great leaders of the day, — to Prescott, Putnam, or Warren, to Stark, Knowlton, or Pomeroy, — and equally those in whose veins flows the kindred blood of any of the brave men who stood together in the battle line.

Insignificant as the conflict seems to us now in regard to the numbers engaged, unimportant as it was then so far as results purely military and strategical were concerned, the valor and patriotism here exhibited, the time when and the opportunity on which they were thus displayed, have justly caused it to be ranked among the decisive battles of the world.

Welcome to the citizens of every State, alike from those which represent the thirteen Colonies, and from the younger States of the Union! We thank them all, whether they come from the great Middle States, which bind us together, from the West, or from the South, for the pilgrimage they have made hither in generous appreciation of the great step that was taken here upon the jagged and thorny path on which we were compelled to walk in our journey toward independence. Fought although this battle was by the men of the colonies of New England, they did not stand for themselves alone, but that there might be founded a structure imperishable as any that man can rear in a free and united government. The corner-stone of the edifice they laid was for all the colonies that were, all the States that are, all the States that are yet to be.

Welcome to the Vice-President of the United States, the Justices of its Supreme Court, and the General commanding its armies! They represent to us the government which was the result of the Revolution. In 1775 Massachusetts was the most populous but one or perhaps two of the colonies, and by the unity of her people the most powerful and warlike of any. She has seen, notwithstanding her own vast increase in population and wealth, although a great State has since been taken from what were then her borders, her relative position change; but she has seen with admiration and not with envy, with pride and satisfaction and not with mean jealousy, the growth of States broader, richer, and fairer than she can hope to be. Whatever changes may have come, her spirit has not changed, her voice has not altered. Then singled out from the colonies to be first subdued and punished, as she lifted her head in stern defence of her ancient liberty, in proud defiance of those who would oppress her, demanding her own great right of local self-government, she called upon her sister colonies for a union that should secure and maintain the rights of all; so to-day she demands for all others every right which she asks for herself, and she calls upon all for that cordial and generous obedience which she is ready to render to the Constitution which has united them forever.

It was to be expected, as the controversy between Great Britain and her colonies moved on from the proposed passage of the Stamp Act, in 1764, and as its inevitable tendency developed, that its weight should be thrown in the first instance upon New England and her chief town and colony. The colonies differed in some important respects in the manner in which they had been settled and in the character of their people. To some there was nothing distasteful in a monarchial government as such, if it had been wisely and liberally administered; but New England remembered always the race from which she sprung, and why her fathers had crossed the sea. Others had come from a love of adventure, from the hope of wealth, from a desire to test the fortunes of a new world; but for none of these things had her founders left the pleasant fields and loved homes of their native land; and the unquenchable love of liberty which animated them lived still in the bosoms of their descendants. Nor was her stern religious faith averse to the assertion by force of what she deemed her liberties. In Parliament, the spirit that prevailed at the time of the accession of George III. was different from that ardent zeal for constitutional freedom which had resulted in the dethronement of James II.; but New England understood her rights, and was prompt to maintain them always in the spirit of the English Commonwealth. "In what book," said one to Selden, "do you find the authority to resist tyranny by force?" and the great lawyer of that day answered, "It is the custom of England, and the custom of England is the law of the land."

It was not the right to tax without representation merely: it was the claim, necessarily involved in such a right, to govern in a different manner, and through officials appointed by the British crown, that astonished the colonies, and united all at first in remonstrance and afterward in determined resistance. Her own character and the circumstances of her situation had placed Massachusetts in the van of this conflict, and had caused her, when the policy of coercion was finally resolved on, to be dealt with by a system of legislation unprecedented in the method usually adopted by Britain in governing her colonies. It was industriously circulated in Parliament that she would not be sustained by the others in the resolute attitude which she had assumed; and upon her were rained in rapid succession the statutes known by the popular names of the Boston Port Bill, the Regulating Act, the Enforcing Act, which were intended to reduce her chief town, the most important in North America, to beggary; which abrogated the provisions of her charter, and took from the people the appointment of their judges, sheriffs, and chief officers;

which forbade the town meetings, whose spirit had been too bold and resolute to be pleasant; which denied to her citizens in many cases the trial by jury, and permitted them to be transported to England or other colonies for trial: a system which, if it could have been enforced, would have reduced her inhabitants to political servitude. Sustained by her own daring spirit, and by the generous encouragement of her sister colonies, she had resisted; and the ten months that had preceded Lexington and Concord had been practically those of war, although blows had not been struck, and blood had not been shed. In the speech of Mr. Burke, delivered March, 1775, upon conciliation with America, memorable not so much for its splendid eloquence (although it is among the masterpieces of the English language) as for its generous statesmanship, he describes Massachusetts, the utter failure of the attempt to reduce her either to submission or anarchy, and her preservation of order even while she rejected the authority of the governor and judges appointed by the British crown. He closes by saying, "How long it will continue in this state, or what may come out of this unheard-of situation, how can the wisest of us conjecture?"

Obviously no such condition of things could endure; and, before his words could cross the Atlantic, the question that he asked had been answered by the appeal to arms. The hoof-beats of Paul Revere's horse along the Lexington road had announced, as the yeomanry of Middlesex, Essex, and Worcester sprang to arms to meet the movement of the British, on the evening of

April 18, from Boston, that the lull was over, and that the storm had come in all its majesty.

The day that followed had changed the relation of the contending parties forever; but the battle of Bunker Hill is also one of the definite steps which mark the progress of the American Revolution. It was not the resistance only of those who will not submit to be oppressed,—it was the result of a distinctly aggressive movement on the part of those who claim the right to levy and maintain armies; nor can I better discharge the duty which has fallen on me, by the deeply regretted absence of the distinguished scholar and orator* who it was hoped would have addressed you, than by recalling its events, even if to some extent I shall seem to trespass upon the domain of the historian or the annalist. The deeds of brave men are their true eulogy; and from a calm contemplation of them we may draw an inspiration and encouragement greater than could be derived from labored argument or carefully studied reflection.

Lexington and Concord had been immediately followed by the gathering of the militia of New England for the siege of Boston, where Gage, now reinforced by Clinton, was compelled to rest, sheltered by the cannon of the ships of war, in command of the garrison of a beleaguered town. The force by which he was thus surrounded was an irregular one, sprung from the ardor and enthusiasm of the people, which far exceeded the means in their power; nor had it any distinctly recognized commander; for while a precedence was accorded

---

* Hon. Robert C. Winthrop.

to General Ward, on account of his seniority, and because more than two-thirds of those assembled were Massachusetts men, as no colony could claim authority over another, it was an army of allies, the troops of each colony being commanded by its own officers, while all the general officers formed a council of war.

The occupation of Bunker Hill was resolved on at the suggestion of the Committee of Safety of Massachusetts, made with knowledge that General Gage was about to take possession of the heights of Dorchester; and on the evening of the 16th of June the force destined for this formidable movement assembled upon the Common at Cambridge. It consisted of some seven or eight hundred men, drawn from the regiments of Prescott, Frye, and Bridge, and some two hundred men of Connecticut, from the regiment of Putnam, under Captain Thomas Knowlton; the whole under the command of Colonel William Prescott. As they formed for their march, Langdon, the President of Harvard College, came from his study, and implored the blessing of God upon their then unknown and dangerous expedition.

So always may the voice of this great institution of learning, which, among their earliest acts and in their day of weakness, our fathers dedicated to the cause of sound learning, seem to be uplifted in solemn invocation above their sons in every struggle, whether in the forum or the field, for progress, for liberty, and for the rights of man! From her halls, then converted into barracks, had come forth the men who, within the thirty-five years that had preceded, had more largely than any others controlled and conducted the great debate between England and her colonies, which, beginning distinctly in 1764 by the proposed passage of the Stamp Act, was now to be settled by the arbitrament of arms. In 1740 had graduated Samuel Adams, and in his thesis for the Master's degree had maintained the proposition which was the foundation of the Revolution, that it was lawful to resist the supreme magistrate, if the Commonwealth could not otherwise be preserved. He had been followed, among others hardly less distinguished, by James Otis, by Cooper and Bowdoin, Hancock and John Adams, by Warren and Quincy. Differing in ages and occupations, in personal qualities and mental characteristics, this remarkable group had been drawn together by a common enthusiasm. To their work they had brought every energy of mind and heart; and they had so managed their share of the controversy, in which all the leading statesmen of Britain had participated, as to have commanded the respect of their opponents, while they inspired and convinced their own countrymen. Many lived to see their hopes fulfilled, yet not all. Already Quincy, the youngest of this illustrious circle, had passed away, appealing with his dying words to his countrymen to be prepared "to seal their faith and constancy to their liberties with their blood." Already the gloomy shadow of mental darkness had obscured forever the splendid powers of Otis; and the hour of Warren was nearly come.

It was nine o'clock in the evening, as the detachments, with Prescott at their head, moved from Cambridge. On arriving at Charlestown, a consultation was held, in which it is believed that Putnam, and perhaps Pomeroy, joined; and it was determined to fortify Breed's Hill,—not then known by the distinctive name it has since borne. Connected with Bunker Hill by a high ridge, these two eminences might not improperly be considered as peaks of the same hill; and, for the purpose of annoyance to the British at Boston, Breed's Hill was better adapted. Together they traverse a large portion of the peninsula of Charlestown, which, connected to the main land by a narrow neck, and, broadening as it approaches Boston, is washed on the northern side by the Mystic, and on the eastern and southern by the Charles river. As the line of retreat to the Neck, which was the only approach, was long, Breed's Hill could not be safely held, however, without fortifying Bunker Hill also.

At midnight work on the redoubt began; and at dawn the entrenchments, as they were discovered by the British fleet in Charles river, which opened upon them at once, were about six feet high. Well sheltered within them, the men, under a terrific cannonade from the ships and floating batteries, aided by a battery on Copp's Hill opposite, continued to labor at the works until about eleven o'clock, when they were substantially finished. At about this time General Putnam reached the field, and recommended that the intrenching tools be sent to Bunker Hill, where he directed the throwing up of a breastwork, which, in the confusion of the day, was never completed.

Oppressed by their severe labor, the terrific heat, and their want of water and provisions, some urged upon Prescott that he should send to General Ward that they might be relieved; but this he resolutely refused, saying that the men who had raised the works were best able to defend them. At Cambridge, however, much anxiety prevailed; and General Ward, who was of opinion that General Gage must attack at once, and would make his principal attack at Cambridge, was unwilling to weaken the main army until his intentions should be developed; but, yielding partially to the energetic remonstrances of the Committee of Safety, through Mr. Richard Devens, consented to order to Charlestown the regiments of Stark and Read, which were under his control.

The consultation at Boston, begun at the announcement made by the cannonade from the British ship, was spirited and long. It was the opinion of Sir Henry Clinton that troops should be landed at the Neck, and the evidently small force upon the hill, then taken in reverse, would easily be captured. But this plan had been rejected by General Gage, as the force thus landed might be placed between two forces of the enemy, in violation of the military axiom that troops should be compelled to deal only with an enemy in front. While the rule is sound, its application in this case might well be doubted, as, by concentrating the fire of the British ships and batteries, it would have been impossible that any organized force could have crossed the Neck, had the British forces landed near this point, and thus imprisoned the Americans in the peninsula.

To attack the works in front, to carry them by main force, to show how little able the rabble that manned them was to compete with the troops of the king, and to administer a stern rebuke that should punish severely those actually in arms, and admonish those whose loyalty was wavering, was more in accordance with the spirit that prevailed in the British army. Its officers were smarting under the disgraceful retreat from Lexington and Concord, and would not yet believe that they had before them foemen worthy of their steel.

It was soon after twelve o'clock when the troops commenced their movements from the North Battery and Long Wharf of Boston, landing at about one o'clock, without molestation, at the extreme point of the peninsula, known as Moulton's Point. On arriving, Major-General Howe, by whom they were commanded, finding the work more formidable than he had anticipated, determined to send for reinforcements. This delay was unwise; for the interval, although it brought him additional troops, proved of far more advantage to the Americans.

When the news of the actual landing arrived at Cambridge, a considerable body of Massachusetts troops was ordered toward Charlestown, while General Putnam ordered forward those of Connecticut. Of all these, however, comparatively few reached the line before the action was decided. Many never reached Charlestown at all; others delayed at Prospect Hill, appalled at the tremendous fire with which the British swept the Neck; while others came no further than Bunker Hill.

It was nearly three o'clock in the afternoon when,

reinforcements having arrived, all was ready in the British line for the attack; and it is time to consider the character of the defences erected, and their position, as well as the forces by which they were then manned. The redoubt, which would inclose the spot where the Monument now stands, was upon the crest of Breed's Hill, an eminence about seventy feet in height. It was about eight rods square, with its front toward the south, overlooking the town and Charles river. Its southeastern angle directly faced Copp's Hill, while its eastern side fronted extensive fields which lay between it and Moulton's Point; Moulton Hill, then about thirty feet in height, but now levelled with the surface of the ground, was situated between it and Moulton's Point. The eastern side of the redoubt was prolonged by a breastwork detached by a sally-port, which extended for about one hundred yards toward a marsh; while the northern side overlooked the Mystic river, from which it was distant about five hundred yards.

For this work the conflict was now about to take place. It had, however, been strengthened upon the side toward the Mystic by a protection without which it would have been untenable; and this addition had been made while General Howe was waiting for reinforcements, by the forethought of Prescott, the skilful conduct of Knowlton, and the fortunate arrival of Stark. Immediately upon the first landing, observing an intention on the part of the British General of moving along the Mystic, and thus attempting to outflank the Americans, Prescott had directed Knowlton, with the Connecticut detachment and with two field-pieces, to oppose them. Captain Knowlton, with his men, who, it will be remembered, were of the original command of Prescott, moved about six hundred feet to the rear of the redoubt upon the side toward the Mystic, and took a position there near the base of Bunker Hill, properly so called, finding a fence which extended toward the Mystic, the foundation of which was of stone, and upon it two rails. Rapidly making, with the materials he found, another fence a few feet distant, he filled the interval with grass from the fields which the mower of yesterday had passed over, but upon which the "great reaper" was to gather to-day a rich harvest. While thus engaged, Stark (a part of whose men were detained at Bunker Hill by Putnam on his proposed works there), followed closely by Read, arrived, and, perceiving instantly the importance of this position for the defence of the intrenchments, — for the way, as he says, for the enemy was "so plain he could not miss it," — extended the line of Knowlton by rails and stones taken from adjoining fences until it reached the river, making on the extreme left on the beach a strong stone wall. As the rail-fence was so far to the rear of the redoubt, there was of course an interval which some slight attempt had been made to close, and where also was posted the artillery of the Americans, which, however, insufficient of itself and feebly served, was of little importance during the action.

In the mean time, few although the reinforcements were, there had now arrived some fresh men to inspire with confidence those who had toiled with Prescott through the weary night and exhausting day without food, drink, or rest. Just before the battle actually commenced, detachments from the Massachusetts regiments of Brewer, Nixon, Woodbridge, Little, and Major Moore, reached the field. Most of these take their place at the breastwork on the left of the eastern front of the redoubt, and a similar breastwork more hastily made by using a cart-way upon the right.

Upon the extreme right were posted a few troops, extending toward the base of the hill, while two flanking parties were thrown out by Prescott to harass the enemy.

A portion of the Massachusetts troops who arrive endeavor to fill the gap which exists between the breastwork and the rail-fence, while yet a few take their stand at the rail-fence. Notably among these latter is the veteran General Pomeroy, of Northampton, too old, as he thinks a few days later, when he is chosen a brigadier by the Continental Congress, to accept so responsible a trust; yet not so old that he cannot fight yet in the ranks, although the weight of seventy years is upon him. Later in the day, when his musket is shattered by a shot, he waves the broken stock in his strong right hand as he directs the men, — a leader's truncheon that tells its own story of the bravery by which it was won. All know the brave old man; and as, declining any command, he takes his place as a volunteer, he is greeted with hearty cheers. To the redoubt has now come Warren, in that spirit of a true soldier, who, having advised against a plan which has been adopted, feels the more called upon to make every effort that it shall succeed. The enthusiasm with which he is received indicates at once the inspiration and encouragement that the men all feel in that gallant presence; but when Prescott offers him the command, he having three days before been appointed a major-general by the Provincial Congress, he declines it, saying, "I come as a volunteer to serve under you, and shall be happy to learn from a soldier of your experience."

The peninsula where the struggle was to take place was in full view across the calm waters of the harbor, and of the Charles and Mystic rivers, whose banks were lined with people, who with mournful and anxious hearts awaited the issue, while each house-top in the town was covered with eager spectators. From Copp's Hill, General Gage, with Burgoyne and Clinton, surrounded by troops, ready themselves to move at an instant's warning, watches the onset of his forces.

The champions are not unworthy of the arena in which they stand. To those who love the "pomp and circumstance" of war, the British troops present a splendid array. The brilliant light flashes back from the scarlet uniforms, the showy equipments, and the glittering arms; and, as they move, there is seen the effect of that discipline whose object is to put at the disposal of the one who commands the strength and courage of the thousands whom he leads. They are of the best and most tried troops of the British army; and some of the regiments have won distinguished honor on the battle-fields of Europe, in the same wars in which the colonies had poured out their blood on this side of the Atlantic in hearty and generous support of the British crown. Their veteran officers are men who have seen service in Europe and America; and their younger officers, like Lord Rawdon and Lord Harris, bear names afterwards distinguished in the chronicles of British warfare. The second in command is Brigadier-General Pigot, slight in person, but known as an officer of spirit and judgment; and their leader, Major-General Howe, bears a name which has been loved and honored in America. The monument which Massachusetts reared in Westminster Abbey to his elder brother, Lord Howe, who fell while leading a column of British and Americans at Ticonderoga in 1758, still stands to inscribe his name among the heroes of England, whose fame is guarded and enshrined within that ancient pile. Above their lines waves the great British ensign, to which the colonies have always looked as the emblem of their country, and with them is the "king's name," which even yet is a tower of strength in the land. As nearly as we can estimate, they number about four thousand men. General Gage's report indicates sufficiently that he does not intend to state the number engaged when he is compelled, later, to acknowledge the casualties of the day.

Upon the other side a different scene presents itself. As the battle is about to open, at the redoubt and upon its flanks are the troops of Massachusetts; at the rail-fence are the troops of Connecticut and those of New Hampshire, with a few men of Massachusetts. How many there were in all cannot be determined with accuracy. Regiments that are frequently spoken of as being present at the engagement were represented by but weak detachments. Towards the close of the battle a few more arrive, but not more than enough to make the place good of the losses that have in the mean time occurred. No judgment can be formed more accurate than that of Washington, who was so soon after with the army, when many of the circumstances were investigated, and whose mature and carefully considered opinion was, that at no time upon our side were more than fifteen hundred men actually engaged.

As we look down the line, there are symptoms everywhere of determination; for such has been the confusion, and so little has been the command which, in their movements, the officers have been able to exercise, that no man is there who does not mean to be there. A few free colored men are in the ranks, who do good service; but it is a gathering almost exclusively of the yeomanry of New England, men of the English race and blood, who stand there that day because there has been an attempt to invade their rights as Englishmen, — rights guaranteed by their charters, and yet older than the Magna Charta itself. There are no uniforms to please the eye; but, as the cowl does not make the monk, so the uniform does not make the soldier, and in their rustic garb they will show themselves worthy of the name before the day is done. No flag waves above their heads; for they are this day without a country, and they fight that they may have one, although they could not have dreamed that the emblem of its sovereignty should float as it now does over millions of freemen from the Atlantic to the far Pacific. The equipments and arms are of all descriptions; but those who carry them know their use, and all, more or less skilled as marksmen, mean, in their stern economy of powder, which is their worst deficiency, that 'every shot shall tell. There is little discipline; but it is not an unwarlike population, and among the men are scattered those who do not look for the first time on the battle-field; and with all is that sense of individual responsibility and duty which to some extent takes its place, — that proud self-consciousness that animates those who know that their own right hands must work their own deliverance. Poorly officered in some respects, — for haste and bad management have put many important posts into inefficient hands, — there are also with them officers who, from experience and ability, might be well counted as leaders on any field. They are New England men, fully understanding those they command, and exercising an influence, by force of their own characters, by their self-devotion and enthusiasm, which cause all around them to yield respectful and affectionate obedience.

Roughly done, the works they have hastily made are yet formidable, the weakest part lying in the imperfectly closed gap between the breastwork and the rail-fence.

At the rail-fence, and on the extreme left, is Stark, distinguished afterwards by the battle of Bennington. He has shown the quick eye and ready hand of the practised soldier by the celerity with which he has extended this line to the Mystic river. Knowlton is there also, still with the Connecticut men, as yet but little reinforced, whose resolute conduct of this day deserves the same eulogy which it received from Washington, when, a year later, he fell gloriously fighting on Harlem Heights at the head of his regiment, — that "it would have been an honor to any country." General Putnam, an officer of tried courage and of energetic character, has come to share in the danger of the assault, now that it is evidently approaching, and is everywhere along this portion of the line, inspiring, encouraging, and sustaining the men. All these, like Pomeroy, are veteran soldiers, who have served in the wars with France and her savage allies; and it is a sundering of old ties to see the British flag up on the other side.

At the redoubt, sustained by Warren, stands the commander of the expedition which has fortified Breed's Hill. He has himself served in the provincial forces of Massachusetts under the British flag, and that so bravely that he has been offered a commission in the regular army, but has preferred the life of a farmer and magistrate in Middlesex. His large and extensive influence he has given to the patriotic cause, and has been recognized from the first as one of those men qualified to command. Powerful in person, with an easy humor which has cheered and inspired with confidence all who are around him, he waits, with a calmness and courage that will not fail him in the most desperate moment, the issue. The hour that he has expected has come; and the gage of battle, so boldly thrown down by the erection of the redoubt, has been lifted.

As the British army moved to the attack, it was in two wings; the first arranged directly to assail the redoubt, and led by Pigot; while the other, commanded by General Howe in person, was divided into two distinct columns, one of which, composed of light infantry, was close to the bank of the river, and intended to turn the extreme left of our line, and with the column in front of the rail-fence to drive the Americans from their position, and cut off the retreat of those in the redoubt.

In the opinion of General Burgoyne, General Howe's "arrangements were soldier-like and perfect;" but the conduct of the battle does not, in a military point, deserve such high commendation. It was clearly an error on the part of General Howe to divide his forces, and make two points of attack instead of one; and an equal error to move up and deploy his columns to fire, in which his troops were at obvious disadvantage, from their want of protection, instead of making an assault without firing. He had failed also to recognize the weak point in the line between the breastwork and the rail-fence, easier to carry than any other point, and, if carried, more certain to involve the whole American force. He had sluggishly permitted the erection of the formidable field-work of the rail-fence, the whole of which had been constructed without any interference subsequent to his arrival on the peninsula; nor, when constructed, does it seem to have occurred to him that, by a floating battery or gunboat stationed in the Mystic river, both of which were within his control, it could have been enfiladed, and the force there dislodged at once.

As the British are seen to advance, the orders are

renewed along the whole American line, in a hundred different forms, not to fire till the enemy are within ten or twelve rods, and then to wait for the word, to use their skill as marksmen, and to make every shot tell. For, although those at the entrenchments and rail-fence act without immediate concert, the scarcity of powder, and the fact that they are without bayonets and can rely only upon their bullets, is known to all. It had been intended to cover the movement of the British by a discharge of artillery; but the balls were, by some mistake of the ordnance officer, found too large for the guns, and afterward, when loaded with grape, it was found impossible to draw them through the miry ground, so that they afforded, in the first assault, no substantial assistance.

The forces of Pigot moved slowly forward, impeded by the heavy knapsacks they had been encumbered with, and by the fences which divided the fields, and continued to fire as they thus advanced. As they got within gunshot, although their fire had done but little damage, our men could not entirely restrain their impatience; but, as some fired, Prescott, sternly rebuking the disorder, appealed to their confidence in him, and some of his officers, springing upon the parapet, kicked up the guns that rested upon it, that they might be sure to wait. This efficient remonstrance had its effect, and the enemy were within ten or twelve rods of the eastern front of the breastworks when the voice of Prescott uttered the words for which every ear was listening, and the stream of fire broke from his line which, by its terrible carnage, checked at once the advance. The attacking lines were old troops, and well led; it was at once sternly returned, but they did not rush on, and in a few moments, wavering and staggering under a fire which was murderous, while their own did little execution, Pigot orders his men to fall back.

In the mean time General Howe, after unsuccessfully endeavoring with a column of light infantry to turn the extreme left of our line on the Mystic, advanced with the grenadiers directly in front of the rail-fence; and somewhat annoyed by the artillery between the breastwork and the rail-fence, which here, directed by Putnam, did its best service, as he approached within eighty or one hundred yards, deployed his forces into line. As at the redoubt, in eagerness, some of our men fired, when the officers threatened to cut down the first man who disobeyed, and, thus rebuked, they restrain themselves until the prescribed distance is reached, when their fire is delivered with such telling effect that, broken and disarranged, the attacking force, alike that directly in front and that upon the banks of the river, recoils before it, while many of the British officers have felt the deadly result of the superiority which the Americans possess as marksmen.

Some minutes, perhaps fifteen, now intervene before the second assault, which are moments of enthusiastic joy in the American lines. All see that they are led by men capable of directing them, that they have rudely hurled back the first onset, and that they are not contending against those who are invincible. As they have seen their enemy turn, some of them at the rail-fence in their eagerness have sprung over it to pursue, but have been restrained by the wisdom of their officers. At the redoubt, Prescott, certain that the enemy will soon re-form and again attack, while he commends the men for their courage and congratulates them for their success, urges them to wait again for his order before they fire. Putnam hastens from the lines, his object being to forward reinforcements, and to arrange, if possible, a new line of defence at Bunker Hill, properly so called, where all was in confusion, the men who had reached there being for the most part entirely disorganized.

The horror of the bloody field is now heightened by the burning of the prosperous town of Charlestown. This had been threatened as early as April 21, by General Gage, if the American forces occupied the town; and the patriotic inhabitants had informed General Ward that they desired him to conduct his military operations without regard to it. Complaining of the annoyance which the sharp-shooters posted along its edges gave to his troops upon the extreme left, General Howe has requested that it be fired, which is done by the cannon from Copp's Hill; it may be also, as was afterwards said, under the impression that his assaulting columns would be covered by its smoke. The smoke was drifted, however, in the other direction; and the provincials beheld without dismay a deed which indicated the ruthless mode in which the war was to be prosecuted. As the enemy advanced to the second assault, their fire was more effective. At the redoubt, Colonels Buckminster, Brewer, and Nixon are wounded; Major Moore mortally. No general result is produced;

and again, as they reach the distance prescribed, the fire of the Americans, directed simultaneously along the whole length of the line, alike of the redoubt and breastwork as well as the rail-fence, is even more destructive than before. Standing the first shock, the enemy continue to advance and fire still; but against so rapid and effective a wave as they now receive, it is impossible to hold their ground, and although their officers, themselves the worst sufferers, are seen frantically summoning them to their duty, all is in vain; they are swept back in complete confusion. General Howe, opposite the rail-fence, is in the fiercest and thickest; left almost alone, as his officers are struck down around him, he is borne along by the current of the retreat rather than directs it.

This time the repulse was terrific. "In front of our works," says Prescott, "the ground was covered with the killed and wounded, many of them within a few yards," while before the rail-fence "the dead," in the homely phrase of Stark, "lay thick as sheep in a fold." Disorder reigned in the British ranks; to stay the rout was for the moment impossible, as many of the companies had entirely lost their officers, and for a short time it seemed that they could not rally again. Had there been a reserve of fresh troops now to advance (which there might have been, had it been possible to organize the scattered detachments which had already reached Bunker's Hill), or even proper support and reinforcement, the conflict would have ended by a victory so complete that perhaps it would have been accepted as putting an end to the British power in America.

Before the third assault some reinforcements reached the rail-fence, especially three Connecticut companies under Major Durkee, and a portion of Gardiner's regiment from Middlesex, the colonel of which was killed during the engagement. A part of this regiment was detained by Putnam on his proposed work at Bunker Hill. The company of Josiah Harris, of Charlestown, took its post at the extreme left of our line at the rail-fence, and won for its native town the honor, when the retreat commenced, of being the last to leave the field.

To the redoubt and breastwork no reinforcements came; and, although the determined and remarkable man who conducted its defence may well have been disappointed at this failure, no word of discouragement escaped his lips. He knew well the duty which as an officer he owed his men, and at another time might have felt that he ought to retreat from a position, the chance of holding which was so slight; yet there was still a chance, and he comprehended fully that on that day it was not a question of strategy or manœuvre, but of the determination and courage of the American people in the assertion of their freedom, which was there bloodily debated. Calm and resolute, cheerful still in outward demeanor, he moved around his lines, assuring his men, "If we drive them back again, they cannot rally;" and, inspired by their confidence in him, they answer enthusiastically, "We are ready."

No supplies of powder have been received, and there are not in his whole command fifty bayonets, so that if the fire shall slacken, and the enemy force their way through it, resistance is impossible. No man has over three rounds of ammunition, and many only two; and, when a few artillery cartridges are discovered, the powder in them is distributed, with the injunction that not a kernel should be wasted.

Discipline, which at such moments will always tell, in perhaps half an hour has done its work among the British troops; and no longer self-confident, but realizing the terrible work before them, the men are throwing off knapsacks for a final and desperate assault. Some have remonstrated; but Sir William, less attractive than his brother, General Lord Howe, less able than his brother, Admiral Lord Howe, who now bears the family title, is a stern soldier, and in personal courage and determination in no way unworthy of the martial race to which he belongs. He feels that his own reputation and that of the soldiers he commands is ruined forever if they sustain defeat at the hands of a band of half-armed rustics. Victory itself will now be attended with mortification enough, after such severe repulses and such terrible losses.

From the other side of the river General Clinton has seen the discomfiture, and, bringing some reinforcements, comes to aid him in rallying his men. Howe has seen, too, what Clinton has also observed, the error of the former disposition of his force, and that the weak point of the American line is between the breastwork and the rail-fence. Toward this and against the redoubt and breastwork he now arranges his next attack. Cannon are brought to bear so as to rake the inside of the breastwork; and, making a demonstration only against the rail-fence that may check any movement upon the flank of his troops, he divides them in three columns.

The two at the left are commanded respectively by Clinton and Pigot, while the right he leads in person. They are to assault together, Clinton upon the left, at the south-eastern angle, and Pigot, upon the eastern front of the redoubt, while Howe's own force is to carry the breastwork, and, striking between it and the rail-fence, bar the way of retreat. Against this formidable array no other preparation could be made by Prescott than to place at the angles of his redoubt the few bayonets at his disposal, and to direct that no man should fire until the enemy were within twenty yards.

The fire of the British artillery, now rendered effective, sweeps the inside of the breastwork, and, no longer tenable, its defenders crowd within the redoubt. Again the voice of Prescott is heard, as the attacking columns approach and are now only twenty yards distant, giving the order to fire. So telling and deadly is the discharge that the front ranks are almost prostrated by it; but, as the fire slackens, the British columns, which have wavered for an instant, move steadily on without returning it. Almost simultaneously upon the three points which are exposed to the assault the enemy reach the little earthwork which so much brave blood has been spent to hold and to gain; and, while they are now so near that its sides already cover them, its commander, determined to maintain it to the last extremity, orders those of his men who have no bayonets to retire to the rear and fire upon the enemy as they mount the parapet.

Those who first ascend are shot down as they scale the works, among them Pitcairn, whose rashness (even if we give him the benefit of the denial he always made of having ordered his soldiers to fire at Lexington) still renders him responsible for the first shedding of blood in the strife. In a few moments, however, the redoubt is half filled by the storming columns; and, although a fierce conflict ensues, it is too unequal for hope, and shows only the courage which animates the men, who, without bayonets, use the butts of their muskets in the fierce effort to stay the now successful assault. As the enemy are closing about the redoubt, if the force is to be extricated from capture, the word to retreat must be given, and reluctantly the brave lips, which have spoken only the words of cheer and encouragement, utter it at last. Already some are so involved that they hew their way through the enemy to join Prescott, and he himself is again and again struck at by the bayonet, of which his clothes give full proof afterward, but defends himself with his sword, the use of which he understands. As our forces leave the redoubt by the entrance on the northern side, they come between the two columns which have turned the breastwork, and the south-eastern angle of the redoubt. These are, however, too much exhausted to use the bayonet effectually, and all are so mingled together that for a few moments the British cannot fire; but as our men extricate themselves the British re-form, and deliver a heavy fire upon them as they retreat.

In the mean time the attack has been renewed upon the rail-fence, but its defenders know well that, if they would save their countrymen at the redoubt, they must hold it resolutely for a few moments longer, and they defend it nobly, resisting every attempt to turn the flank. They see soon that Prescott has left the hill, that the intrenchments are in the hands of the enemy at last; and, their own work gallantly done, they retreat in better order than could have been expected of troops who had so little organization, and who looked for the first time on a battle-field. Upon the crest of Bunker Hill (properly so called) General Putnam, with the confused forces already there, gallantly struggles to organize a line and make a new stand, but without success. Our forces recross the Neck and occupy Ploughed Hill, now Mount Benedict, at its head; but there is no disposition on the part of the British to pursue, for the terrible slaughter too well attests the price at which the nominal victory has been obtained.

The loss of the British, according to General Gage's account, was in killed and wounded ten hundred and fifty-four, and it was generally believed that this was understated by him. There was inducement enough to do this; for so disastrous was his despatch felt to be that the government hesitated to give it to the public, until forced to do so by the taunts of those who had opposed the war, and the method by which it had been provoked.

Sir William Howe seemed to have borne that day a charmed life; for, while ten officers of his staff were among the killed and wounded, he had escaped substantially uninjured. His white silk stockings, draggled with the crimson stain of the grass, wet with the blood of his men, attested that he had kept the promise made to them on the beach, that he should ask no man to go further than he was prepared to lead.

On the American side the loss, as reported by the Committee of Safety, was in killed and wounded four hundred and forty-nine,—by far the larger part of these casualties occurring in the capture of the redoubt, and after the retreat commenced. Prescott, who, in the hours that had passed since he left Cambridge, had done for the independence of his country work that the greatest might well be satisfied with doing in a lifetime, was unhurt; but as the retreat commenced Warren had fallen, than whom no man in America could have been more deeply deplored.

Massachusetts in her Congress, and the citizens of all the colonies, united in doing honor to his heroic self-sacrifice, and pure, noble fame; but no eulogy was more graceful than that of Mrs. John Adams, herself one of the most interesting figures of the Revolution, or more touching than that of the warm-hearted Pomeroy, who lamented the caprice of that fortune which had spared him in the day of battle, an old war-worn soldier whose work was nearly done, and taken Warren in the brightness of his youth, and with his vast capacity to serve his country. Yet for him who shall say it was not well; there are many things in life dearer than life itself: honor in its true and noble sense, patriotism, duty, all are dearer: to all these he had been faithful. His position is forever among the heroes and martyrs of liberty,—his reward forever in the affection of a grateful people. As the dead always bear to us the image which they last bore when on earth, and as by the subtle power of the imagination we summon before us the brave who stood here for their country, that noble presence, majestic in its manly beauty, seems to rise again, although a hundred years are gone, with all the fire of his burning eloquence, with all the ardor of his patriotic enthusiasm, with all the loftiness of his generous self-devotion. So shall it seem to rise, although centuries more shall pass, to inspire his countrymen in every hour of doubt and trial with a valor and patriotism kindred to his own.

The story I have told, fellow-citizens, has been often related before you far more vividly; nor has it been in my power to add anything to the facts which patient and loving investigation has long since brought to light. Tested by the simple rule that whoever holds or gains the ground fought for wins the victory, the battle was, of course, at its close, a defeat for the provincial forces; but it was a defeat that carried and deserved to carry with it all the moral consequences of a victory. As General Burgoyne gazed from Copp's Hill on the scene which he so graphically describes in a letter to Lord Stanley, he was saddened, he says, "by the reflection that a defeat would be perhaps the loss of the British empire in America;" but, although in his eyes a victory, it was one which equally marked the loss of that empire.

The lesson drawn from it was the same both in Europe and America. "England," wrote Franklin, "has lost her colonies forever;" and Washington, as he listened with intense interest to the narrative, and heard that the troops he was coming to command had not only withstood the fire of the regulars, but had again and again repulsed them, renewed his expressions of confidence in final victory.

In England the news was received with mortification and astonishment; no loss in proportion to the number engaged had ever been known so serious; and in the excited debates of the Parliament it was afterwards alleged to have been caused by the misbehavior of the troops themselves. The charge was certainly unjust; for, whatever may be thought of his own management, the troops he had directed deserved the praise that General Gage gave them when he said, " British valor had never been more conspicuous than in this action." From his eyes the scales seemed to have fallen at last; and closely beleaguered still, even after the victory he claimed, he acknowledged that the people of New England were not " the despicable rabble they had sometimes been represented," and recognized that an offensive campaign here was not possible.

The shrewd Count Vergennes, who, in the hour of the humiliation of France by the loss of her colonial possessions, had predicted that she would be avenged by those whose hands had largely wrought it, and that as the colonies no longer needed the protection of Great Britain they would end by shaking off all dependence upon her, was now the French Minister of Foreign Affairs, and keenly remarked that " if it won two more such victories as it had won at Bunker Hill, there would be no British army in America."

The battle of Bunker Hill had consolidated the Revolution. Had the result been different; had it been shown that the hasty, ill-disciplined levies of New England could not stand before the troops of the king (or the ministerial troops, as our official documents called them); had the easy victory over them, which had been foolishly promised, been weakly conceded, — the cause of independence might have been indefinitely postponed. Nay, it is not impossible that armed resistance might for the time have ended, and that other colonies not so deeply involved in the contest might have extricated themselves, each making such terms as it pleased or as it could. But the coolness and splendid valor with which the best troops then known had been met, the repulses which they had again and again encountered, the bloody and fearful cost at which they had finally carried the coveted point, that their opponents had yielded only when ammunition utterly failed — had shown that the yeomanry of New England were the true descendants of that race who, on the battle-fields of England, had stood against and triumphed over King Charles and his cavaliers. "New England alone," said John Adams, "can maintain this war for years." He was right; the divisions that existed elsewhere were practically unknown here; no matter what colonies hesitated or doubted, her path was straightforward, and her goal was independence. While her colonies deferred to the Continental Congress the form of government they should adopt, each had taken into its own hands all the powers that rightfully belong to sovereign States, and exercised them through its provincial Congress and its committees. Heartily desiring and eagerly looking forward to a union of the colonies, she had settled that in her local affairs she was competent to govern herself: this she had maintained that day in arms, and her period of vassalage was over.

Willingly would I pursue the theme further; but the limits which custom prescribes for an address of this nature are too narrow to permit this. You know well the years of doubt, anxiety, and struggle that succeeded; but before we part something should be said of those that have passed since their triumphant close.

I have forborne to speak of the causes which led to the American Revolution. They have recently been so carefully and ably analyzed by the distinguished orators who aided in the celebrations at Concord and Lexington, that I have preferred to devote a few moments to a consideration of some of its effects, by which the propriety and wisdom of such a movement in human affairs must always be eventually tested.

That the formation and adoption of the Constitution of the United States has been to us, since our independence was finally achieved, the great event of the century, must be universally conceded. It was the great good fortune and the crowning triumph of the statesmen who guided us through the Revolution, that they lived long enough to embody its results in a permanent and durable form; for it is harder to secure the fruits of a victory than to win the victory itself. Many a day of triumph upon the field has been but a day of carnage and of empty glory, barren in all that was valuable; and the victories that have been won upon the political field are no exceptions to the rule, with which history teems with illustrations.

Our ancient ally, whose services during the last years of our war were of so much value to our exhausted treasury and armies, and whose gift of the generous and chivalric Lafayette at its opening was almost equally precious, passed a few years later than we through its own desperate struggle; yet, although that fierce tide swept in a sea of fire and blood over all the ancient institutions of the monarchy, how impossible it has proved to this day for France to supply the place of the government which it so sternly overthrew with one thoroughly permanent, giving peace and security! Republic, Directory, Consulate, Empire, Kingdom, have had their turn; dynasty after dynasty, faction after faction, have asserted their sway over her.

For a government under the constitutions of the several States, and under that of the United States, this people was prepared alike by its previous history, and by that which followed its separation from Britain. It was the legitimate outgrowth of experience, and not a government framed, like those of the Abbé Siéyes at the end of their revolution for the French, by the aid of philosophic speculation, and on the basis of that which should be, and not of that which was. While the colonies, by means of their representative and legislative systems, had been accustomed to deal with their local affairs, and impose their local taxation, and had successfully resisted the attempt to interfere with these rights, yet, from the relation they had also been accustomed to sustain toward Britain, it was not to them a novel idea that two governments, each complete and supreme within its sphere, might coexist, the one controlling the local affairs of each individual State, while the other exercised its powers over all in their intercourse with each other and with foreign nations.

Painfully conscious of their weakness, the desire for a union of all had gone hand in hand with the desire of each to preserve its own separate organization. The first Continental Congress had not exercised political authority; it had assembled only on behalf of the United Colonies to petition and remonstrate against the various arbitrary acts of the British government. Those which followed, however, with patriotic courage had boldly seized the highest powers; yet, as they could exercise such powers only so far as each State gave its assent and sustained them, the necessary result followed that their decrees were often but feebly executed, and sometimes utterly disregarded. Later in the war the Confederation had followed, by which it had been sought to fix more definitely the relation of the States by giving more determinate authority to the Congress, and to rescue the country from the financial ruin which had overtaken it.

But the powers of the Congress of the Confederation, like those of the Continental Congress, were such as were consistent only with a league of sovereign and independent States, and were in their exercise less efficacious, because they had been carefully defined and limited. The Confederation did not constitute a government; it did not assume to act upon the people, but upon the several States; and upon them no means existed of enforcing its requisitions and decrees, or of compelling them to the performance of the treaties it might make, or the obligations it might incur. Among allied powers, from the nature of the case, there is no mode of enforcing the agreement of alliance except by war.

The great work of achieving independence had, however, been completed by the Confederation in spite of all its weakness and inherent defects. These were, however, more clearly seen when the sense of an immediate and common danger, and the cohesive pressure of war, were withdrawn. A mere aggregation of States could not take its place among the peoples of the world. A national sovereignty was needed, capable of establishing a financial system of its own, of raising money for its own support by taxation or regulations of trade, of forming treaties with sufficient power to execute them, of insuring order in every State, of bringing each State into proper relations with the others, and able, if need be, to declare war or maintain peace, — a sovereignty which should act directly on the people themselves in the exercise of all its rightful powers, and not through the intervention of the States.

The years of unexampled depression which followed peace with Britain were not attributable only to the exhaustion of war: the impossibility of establishing a financial or a commercial system, the sense of insecurity that prevailed, paralyzed industry and enterprise. Already jarrings and contests between the several States presaged the danger which had destroyed the republics of Greece and those of Italy during the Middle Ages; already civil discord, which, although suppressed, had thrown the State temporarily into confusion, had made its appearance in Massachusetts; already doubts began to be expressed, even by some who had been ardent in the patriot cause, whether they had been wise to separate from a government which, even if monarchical, was strong and able to defend and protect its subjects; and it had come to be realized that there must be somewhere a controlling power competent to maintain peace between the States, and to guarantee to each the security of its own government.

The Convention which met at Philadelphia in 1787 gave these States a government, and made them a nation; and while I know to that which is impersonal there is wanting much of the ardor that personal loyalty inspires, yet, so far as there may be warmth in the devotion we cherish for an institution, it should awaken at the mention of the Constitution of the United States. The noble preamble declares by whom it is made, and defines its purposes: "We, the people of the United States, in order to form a more perfect union, establish justice, insure domestic tranquillity, provide for the common defence, promote the general welfare, and secure the blessings of liberty to ourselves and our posterity, do ordain and establish this Constitution for the United States of America." In the largest measure it has fulfilled these objects; and the judgment and far-seeing wisdom with which its founders met the difficulties before them more and more challenge our admiration as the years advance and the republic extends.

Formed by men who differed widely in their views, — some who clung resolutely still to the idea that it was dangerous to the liberties of the States to constitute an efficient central power, and others who, like Hamilton, preferred a consolidated government whose model should be the British Constitution, — it might easily have been that a government so framed should have been a patchwork of incongruities, whose discordant and irreconcilable provisions would have revealed alternately the influence of either opinion. Yet, differing although they did, they were statesmen still; and, educated in the rough school of adversity and trial, they realized that a government must be constructed capable alike of daily efficient practical operation, and of adapting itself to the constantly varying exigencies in which sovereign States must act. How doubtful they were of their success, how nobly they succeeded in the government they made, to-day we know.

We have seen its vast capacity for expansion as it has received under the shield, on which are emblazoned the arms of the Union, State after State, as it has arisen in what was on the day of its formation the untrodden wilderness, and advanced to the blessings of liberty and civilization; we have recognized the flexibility it possesses in leaving to States materially differing in local characteristics and interests the control and management of their immediate affairs; and we have known its capacity to vindicate itself in the wildest storm of civil commotion.

Let us guard this Union well; for as upon it all that is glorious in the past is resting, so upon it all our hopes of the future are founded. Let us demand, of those who are to administer its great powers, purity, disinterestedness, devotion to well-settled, carefully considered principles and convictions. Let us cherish the homely but manly virtues of the men who for it met the storm of war in behalf of a government and a country; their simple faith in what was just and right, that found its root in their unswerving belief in something higher than mere human guidance. Let us encourage that universal education, that diffusion of knowledge, which everywhere oppose themselves as barriers, steadily and firmly, alike to plunder and fraud, to disorder and turbulence. Above all, let us strive to maintain and renew the fraternal feeling which should exist between all the States of the Union.

We will not pretend that the trial through which we have passed has faded either from our hearts or memories; yet no one will, I trust, believe that I would rudely rake open the smouldering embers that all would gladly wish to see extinguished forever, or that, deeply as I feel our great and solemn obligations to those who preserved and defended the Union, I would speak one word except with respect and in kindness even to those who assailed it, yet who have now submitted to its power.

In the Union two classes of States had their place differing radically in this, that in the one the system of slavery existed. It was a difficulty which the fathers could not eliminate from the problem before them. They dealt with it with all the wisdom and foresight they possessed. Strongly impressed in their belief of the equal rights of man, — for their discussions had compelled them to deal with fundamental principles, — they were not so destitute of philosophy that they did not see that what they demanded for themselves should be accorded to others; and, believing that the whole system would fade before the noble influence of free government as a dark cloud melts and drifts away, they watched, and with jealous care, that when that day came the instrument they signed should bear no trace of its existence. It was not thus to be, and the system has passed away in the tempest of battle and amid the clang of arms.

The conflict is over, the race long subject is restored to liberty, and the nation has had "under God a new birth of freedom." No executions, no harsh punishments, have sullied the conclusion; day by day the material evidences of war fade from our sight, the bastions sink to the level of the ground which surrounded them, scarp and counter-scarp meet in the ditch which divided them. So let them pass away forever. The contest is marked distinctly only by the changes in the organic laws of the Constitution, which embody in more definite forms the immortal truths of the Declaration of Independence. That these include more than its logical and necessary results cannot fairly be contended. Did I believe that they embraced more than these, did I find in that great instrument any changes which should place or seek to place one State above another, or above another class of States, so as to mark a victory of sections or localities, I could not rejoice, for

I should know that we had planted the seeds of "unnumbered woes."

To-day it is the highest duty of all, no matter on what side they were, but, above all, of those who have struggled for the preservation of the Union, to strive that it become one of generous confidence, in which all the States shall, as of old, stand shoulder to shoulder, if need be, against the world in arms. Toward those with whom we were lately in conflict, and who recognize that the results are to be kept inviolate, there should be no feeling of resentment or bitterness. To the necessity of events they have submitted; to the changes in the Constitution they have assented; we cannot and we do not think so basely or so meanly of them as to believe that they have done so except generously and without mental reservation.

We know that it is not easy to readjust all the relations of society when one form is suddenly swept away; that the sword does its work rudely, and not with that gradual preparation which attends the changes of peace. We realize that there are difficulties and distrusts not to be removed at once between those who have been masters and slaves; yet there are none which will not ultimately disappear. All true men are with the South in demanding for her peace, order, honest and good government, and encouraging her in the work of rebuilding all that has been made desolate. We need not doubt the issue; she will not stand as the "Niobe of nations," lamenting her sad fate; she will not look back to deplore a past which cannot and should not return; but with the fire of her ancient courage she will gird herself up to the emergencies of her new situation, she will unite her people by the bonds of that mutual confidence which their mutual interests demand, and renew her former prosperity and her rightful influence in the Union.

Fellow-citizens, we stand to-day on a great battle-field in honor of the patriotism and valor of those who fought upon it. It is the step which they made in the world's history we would seek to commemorate; it is the example which they have offered us we would seek to imitate. The wise and thoughtful men who directed this controversy knew well that it is by the wars personal ambition has stimulated, by the armies whose force has been wielded alike for domestic oppression or foreign conquest, that the sway of despots has been so widely maintained. They had no love for war or any of its works, but they were ready to meet its dangers in their attachment to the cause of civil and religious liberty. They desired to found no Roman republic, "whose banners, fanned by conquest's crimson wing," should float victorious over prostrate nations, but one where the serene beauty of the arts of peace should put to shame the strifes that have impoverished peoples and degraded nations. To-day let us rejoice in the liberty which they have gained for us; but let no utterances but those of peace salute our ears, no thoughts but those of peace animate our hearts.

Above the plains of Marathon, even now, as the Grecian shepherd watches over his flocks, he fancies that the skies sometimes are filled with lurid light, and that in the clouds above are re-enacted the scenes of that great day when, on the field below, Greece maintained her freedom against the hordes who had assailed her. Again seem to come in long array, "rich with barbaric pearl and gold," the turbaned ranks of the Persian host, and the air is filled with the clang of sword and shield, as again the fiery Greek seems to throw himself upon and drive before him his foreign invader; shadows although all are that flit in wild, confused masses along the spectral sky.

Above the field where we stand, even in the wildest dream, may no such scenes offend the calmness of the upper air, but may the stars look forever down upon prosperity and peace, upon the bay studded with its white-winged ships, upon the populous and far extending city, with its marts of commerce, its palaces of industry, its temples, where each man may worship according to his own conscience; and, as the continent shall pass beneath their steady rays, may the millions of happy homes attest a land where the benign influence of free government has brought happiness and contentment, where labor is rewarded, where manhood is honored, and where virtue and religion are revered!

Peace forever with the great country from which the day we commemorate did so much rudely to dissever us! If there were in that time, or if there have been since, many things which we could have wished otherwise, we can easily afford to let them pass into oblivion. But we do not forget in the struggle of the Revolution how many of her statesmen stood forth to assert the justice of our cause, and to demand for us the rights of which we had been deprived until the celebrated address was passed which declared that the House of Commons would consider as enemies to the king and country all those who would further attempt the prosecution of a war on the continent of America for the purpose of reducing the American colonies to obedience.

From her we have drawn the great body of laws which, modified and adapted to our different situation, protect us to-day in our property, its descent, possession, and transmission, and which guard our dearer personal rights by the *habeas corpus* and the trial by jury. They were our countrymen who from the days of King John to those of George III. have made of her a land in which "freedom has broadened slowly down from precedent to precedent."

It was she that had placed her foot upon the "divine right of kings," and solemnly maintained that governments exist only by consent of the governed, when, in 1688, she changed the succession to the British crown, and caused her rulers to reign thereafter by a statute of Parliament.

From her we learned the great lessons of constitutional liberty which as against her we resolutely asserted. There was no colony of any other kingdom of Europe that would have dreamed of demanding as rights those things which our fathers deemed their inheritance as Englishmen, none that would not have yielded unhesitatingly to any injunction of the parent State. Whatever differences have been or may hereafter come, let us remember still that we are the only two great distinctly settled free governments, and that the noble English tongue in which we speak alike is "the language of freemen throughout the world."

Above all, may there be peace forever among the States of this Union! "The blood spilt here," said Washington upon the place where we stand, "roused the whole American people, and united them in defence of their rights,—that Union will never be broken." Prophecies may be made to work their own fulfilment; and, whatever may have been our trials and our difficulties, let us spare no efforts that this shall be realized. Achieving our independence by a common struggle, endowed to-day with common institutions, we see even more clearly than before that the States of this Union have before them a common destiny.

We have commenced here in Massachusetts the celebration of that series of events which made of us a nation; and let each, as it approaches in the centennial cycle, serve to kindle anew the fires of patriotism. Let us meet on the fields where our fathers fought, and where they lie, whether they fell with the stern joy of victory irradiating their countenances, or in the gloomy hours of disaster and defeat. Alike in remembrance of Saratoga and Yorktown, and of the dreary winter of Valley Forge, at Trenton and Princeton, and at the spots immortalized in the bloody campaign of the Jerseys, at King's Mountain and Charleston, at Camden and Guilford Court House, and along the track of the steadily fighting, slowly retreating Greene through the Carolinas.

Above all, at the city from which went forth the Declaration that we were, and of right ought to be, a free and independent nation, let us gather, and, by the sacred memories of the great departed, pledge ourselves to transmit untarnished the heritage they have left us.

The soldiers of the Revolution are gone, the statesmen who embodied their work in the Constitution of the United States have passed away. With them, too, sleep those who in the earlier days watched the development of this wondrous frame of government.

The mighty master of thought and speech, by whose voice fifty years ago was dedicated the Monument at whose base we stand, and whose noble argument that the Constitution is not a compact, but a law, by its nature supreme and perpetual, won for him the proud name of the Expounder of the Constitution, rests with those whose work he so nobly vindicated, happy at least that his eyes were not permitted to behold the sad sight of States "discordant, belligerent, and drenched in fraternal blood."

The lips of him who twenty-five years ago commemorated this anniversary with that surpassing grace and eloquence all his own, and with that spirit of pure patriotism in which we may strive at least to imitate him, are silent now. Throughout the cruel years of war that clarion voice, sweet yet far-resounding, summoned his countrymen to the struggle on which our Union depended; yet the last time that it waked the echoes of the ancient hall dedicated to liberty, even while the retiring storm yet thundered along the horizon, was, as he would have wished it should have been, in love and charity to the distressed people of the South.

But, although they have passed beyond the veil which

separates the unseen world from mortal gaze, the lessons which they have left remain, adjuring us whatever may have been the perils, the discords, the sorrows of the past, to struggle always for that "more perfect Union" ordained by the Constitution. Here, at least, however poor and inadequate for an occasion that rises so vast and grand above us our words may be, none shall be uttered that are not in regard and love to all of our fellow-citizens, no feelings indulged except those of anxious desire for their prosperity and happiness.

Beside those of New England, we are gratified to-day by the presence of military organizations from New York and Pennsylvania, from Maryland, Virginia, and South Carolina, as well as by that of distinguished citizens from these and other States of the Union. Their fathers were ancient friends of Massachusetts; it was the inspiration they gave which strengthened the heart and nerved the arm of every man of New England. In every proper and larger sense the soil upon which their sons stand to-day is theirs as much as ours; and, wherever there may have been estrangement, here at least we have met upon common ground. They unite with us in recognition of the great principles of civil and religious liberty, and in pious memory of those who vindicated them; they join with us in the wish to make of this regenerated Union a power grander and more august than its founders dared to hope.

Standing always in generous remembrance of every section of the Union, neither now nor hereafter will we distinguish between States or sections in our anxiety for the glory and happiness of all. To-day upon the verge of the centuries, as together we look back upon that which is gone in deep and heartfelt gratitude for the prosperity so largely enjoyed by us, so together will we look forward serenely and with confidence to that which is advancing. Together we will utter our solemn aspirations in the spirit of the motto of the city which now incloses within its limits the battle-field and the town for which it was fought: "As God was to our fathers, so may He be to us!"

The orator was listened to with close attention, and was frequently applauded. At the conclusion, Hon. E. R. Hoar proposed three cheers for General Devens, which, under the lead of the Marshal, were heartily given.

Afterwards, the Apollo Club sung the following hymn, written by CHARLES JAMES SPRAGUE: —

>Here, where the savage bands
>Roved through the forest lands,
>   Wild and unknown,
>Came sturdy men of yore,
>Strong in the faith they bore,
>Making this desert shore
>   Freedom's high throne.

>Here, where the pilgrim few
>Unto a nation grew,
>   Spread far and wide,
>Came an invading foe,
>That throne to overthrow
>With but a feeble blow
>   Struck at our pride.

>   Here, where the patriots stood,
>   Came that wild strife of blood,
>   Where peace now reigns.
>   Here hand to hand they met,
>   Here then our soil was wet
>   With the red tide that yet
>   Throbs in our veins.
>
>   Gone is the savage now,
>   Gone the invading foe,
>   Freed is our land.
>   O Lord of war and peace,
>   May strife forever cease,
>   And may our strength increase,
>   Fed by Thy hand!

Judge WARREN then advanced, and, gracefully acknowledging the applause which greeted him, addressed the audience as follows: —

ADDRESS BY G. WASHINGTON WARREN, PRESIDENT OF THE ASSOCIATION.

This is the first centennial anniversary of Bunker Hill. The century just past has presented to its successors yonder national Monument of gratitude to the heroic fathers of the republic. Erected under the supervision of Solomon Willard, that renowned architect, who spurned to take the proper compensation for his eighteen years' service, being a descendant of a gallant officer whose remains lie at the foot of this hill; consecrated at its commencement and completion by the majestic Webster, whose words still live, and can never fail to instruct; impelled in its progress by the silver-voiced, all-persuasive Everett — the contribution of the whole people, to which Louisiana, South Carolina, and the other States joined with Massachusetts, it stands the silent orator, gathering, in its massive form, all the time-hallowed associations of the place; and, as it lifts its gray head to keep company with the stars, and takes notes as impassively as they of the centuries that are to follow, may it be to all the inhabitants to the remotest age an INSPIRATION to patriotism, and to those good works which make for the liberty, the union, and the true grandeur of the United States of America.

The Association invoked the presence of the high officers of the National Government in its three co-ordinate departments, and of the Executive officer of every State, and of the principal city thereof. From the sincere regrets of the absent we know that all are here either in the body or in spirit. The heart of Bunker Hill, now crowning the metropolis of Boston, is big enough to receive you all, and begs you in her name and in her undying glories to bury all animosities, and to resolve that henceforth there shall be no contention except who shall best serve our glorious country.

We desired also that every nation should be represented here by its minister accredited to Washington, making this an occasion also of international harmony. Yes, we desired very much to be honored by the presence of the distinguished minister from our mother country, whose good sovereign is nowhere more highly esteemed than here. In 1871, Great Britain and the United States celebrated this anniversary by the following the motto of President Grant, "Let us have peace."

The battle of Bunker Hill was fought by our fathers in defence of the principles of the British constitution, and the issue has been for the healing of all nations.

At the Bunker Hill dinner, fifty years ago, Lafayette predicted that the toast on this Centennial day would be To ENFRANCHISED EUROPE. How far this prediction has been verified, let the emancipation of the serfs in Russia, the re-establishment of the republic in France, the enlargement of the suffrage in England, and the general spread of liberal principles and the encouragement of learning everywhere, answer.

South Carolina has sent us a palmetto tree, which we have planted in front by the side of the pine tree. May those two State emblems to-day planted on Bunker Hill be a symbol of renewed fraternity, never again to be interrupted. Let it be taken also as a pledge of reunion between all the States; for, with Massachusetts and South Carolina in full accord, as they were one hundred years ago, our Union is as firm and enduring as our Monument, which they, with true patriotism, joined together in building.

In calling upon some of our distinguished guests to address you briefly, I will take the liberty to present to you first the gallant General who has travelled fifteen hundred miles to participate in this celebration.

REMARKS OF GENERAL SHERMAN.

Mr. President, Ladies and Gentlemen: — Before responding to your call, let me take issue with your honored President in calling on me as the National Representative. You can see for yourselves on this platform the Vice-President of the United States, several Judges of the Supreme Court, and about a dozen Governors of States, all of whom take precedence of me, and all of whom are accustomed to speak and are expecting to address you. Still it is true that I have come about fifteen hundred miles to share in this grand Centennial, and I am glad that I have come.

If I do nothing else, I can be the first to respond to General Devens' call, to come on this platform and renew the pledge to maintain and defend the Constitution of our country, to fight again, if need be, for the old flag and those sacred principles of right that were announced ninety-nine years ago by your Hancock and the Adamses. I know that there are many soldiers in this vast audience, and, were I to call on them to come forward and share in this pledge, I am sure they would promptly respond with an amen.

Indeed do we stand on sacred soil at the foot of old Bunker Hill Monument. I almost feel pained to hear it called Breed's Hill. It was Bunker Hill when I was a boy, and to me it is Bunker Hill still. I find it recorded in bold letters on that granite shaft, and I insist that *it is* Bunker Hill. If Mr. Breed is here, I advise him to convey to Bunker, and be content with the other and larger hill close by.

I assure you that I have listened with the most intense interest to the graphic description by your orator, General Devens, of that battle, fought on this ground one hundred years ago, and confess to a soldier's admiration of that small band, under Colonel Prescott, that was "told off" in the camp at Cambridge, to go, they knew not exactly where, to fight the veteran British host beleaguered in Boston. They marched off silently by night to do, as soldiers should, their duty; and it was providential that they were conducted to this very spot, instead of the one further back, designated in their orders. I have no doubt that General Devens has truthfully given the narration, with a fair distribution of the honors.

Warren, though the senior present, did not assume, as he might have done, the supreme command, but fought as a volunteer, and died upon the field a martyr and a hero, venerated everywhere.

Prescott was the actual commander on this spot. He conducted his brigade, prepared with their intrenching tools, and with their weapons to fight. Silently and with skill they constructed by night the redoubt and flank defences, and the daylight found them ready for the issue. How they fought you have already heard, and, as the actual commander on Bunker Hill, Prescott is entitled to all honor and glory.

General Putnam, too, contributed large assistance; but he has ample honor without claiming this. I like to think of him in that story of a man riding down the fabulous stairs pictured in our story-books, at some place, I confess I now forget where. He was a glorious old soldier, and his services and examples are worth a dozen monuments like this on Bunker Hill, even if made of pure gold.

Now, ladies and gentlemen, I have responded to your call, not with any purpose to edify you, but because you seem to desire it; and, though a stranger to most of you, I believe you desire to simply look upon and hear from one of those who have flitted across the horizon and attracted some notice; but I also thank you for your cordial reception, and for giving me the opportunity to witness one of the most gorgeous pageants that has ever occurred on this continent.

Seated by thousands beneath this vast canopy, you doubtless esteem yourselves a vast and well-ordered crowd; but you are as nothing compared with the hosts which to-day lined the streets of Boston. You hardly equal the group which occupied each block of the hundreds along which we have passed to-day; and as the newspapers of the morning will describe to them, and to all the world, what occurs here, I will no longer occupy your time, but give place to the many orators that will be proud to address such an audience. I again thank you for your kind and cordial reception, and apologize for detaining you so long.

The President then said: — "There is a little time left. I propose to call upon all the Governors, beginning with the Governor who has come farthest to see us. All Governors will take notice thereof and *govern* themselves accordingly."

The Governor of Mississippi and the Governor of Michigan were called, but neither responded. The Governor of Pennsylvania was next called for, and upon presenting himself was greeted with three cheers.

REMARKS OF GOVERNOR HARTRANFT.

Ladies and Gentlemen: — I certainly feel a delicacy in appearing before you as a Governor, because I was reminded to-day that Governors were as plenty in this town as general officers were at Washington during the war, and certainly I suppose some of those other gentlemen are now in the field doing duty. I did not come fifteen hundred miles, like my friend General Sherman, but I have brought with me fifteen hundred Pennsylvanians to take part in this celebration. It is not my desire to make any speech, but I know they would not like it did I not invite you from all States in the Union, and pledge you a cordial welcome to Philadelphia next year, when the hundredth anniversary of our nation is to be celebrated. [The PRESIDENT. — "We are coming."] The celebration is, of course, of a national character, and we in common only have our share in the ceremonies and in the exhibition. But we also have a local interest and pride in having every citizen, whether he comes from the North or the South, the East or the West, feel assured that he will receive all the hospitality that it is in our power to extend, and that we meet there as brothers and freemen around those famed precincts where the charters of our liberties were signed. Let us there bury our differences and our animosities, resolving to perpetuate and transmit, unimpaired and indivisible, the Union which has been given to us.

The Apollo Club then sung the following song, written by CHARLES JAMES SPRAGUE: —

Freedom dwells throughout our own beloved land;
 Up to heaven its voice is swelling;
From the mountain heights afar to ocean strand
 Every breeze the tale is telling.
Never weary of the ever joyous song,
Heart and voice united bear along.
  Loyal to the end,
  Ready to defend,
 Foe within and out repelling.

War's alarum rolled a hundred years ago
 O'er the peaceful scene around us;
Where our patriot fathers struck a mortal blow
 At the haughty power that bound us.
Now from north or south together e'er we stand,
Dwellers in a free and mighty land.
  Loyal to the end,
  Ready to defend,
 What their gloried valor found us.

Freedom dwells throughout our own beloved land,
 Wide as heaven arches o'er it;
Like the rising sun, the patriot's armed hand
 Swept the clouds of wrong before it.
Sound aloud the joyous word from crag to crag!
Plant on every peak our starry flag!
  Loyal to the end,
  Ready to defend,
 Guard, and, as a shrine, adore it!

The President next called upon the Governor of New Jersey, who responded as follows: —

REMARKS OF GOVERNOR BEDLE.

This is no time, ladies and gentlemen, to undertake to make a speech. On receiving the invitation to be present on this occasion, I determined, if it were possible, as an humble representative of the State of New Jersey, to come here and join in this celebration; and it is a happy moment for me to be here, in the home of the Adamses and of Hancock, two of whom, Samuel Adams and John Hancock, were rebels, in the estimation of Great Britain, of the deepest dye, and, when others were to be pardoned, their crimes were such as to merit only condign punishment. They were not rebels, they were patriots; they were freemen; they were raised up by Providence to assert the great principles that were afterwards fought for at the battle of Bunker Hill and proclaimed in the Declaration of Independence.

I am here from New Jersey. New Jersey, too, has a history. I am here not to praise her. She has her record. She has her Trenton, her Princeton, and her Monmouth, and in due time those events will be celebrated, and then we expect Massachusetts will be there. We expect to be at that great centennial of July 4th, 1876, which is to be the grand consummation of all the centennials; and when you go across the territory of New Jersey remember that the winter of 1776 was "the time that tried men's souls" there. You know how our gallant American army, after evacuating New York, retreated across the State of New Jersey; how they were followed by the British army; how they were re-formed, and how, when those battles of Trenton and Princeton were fought, the depressed spirit of our forefathers revived and the tide of revolution turned.

Now, my friends, I have nothing more to say, except

to thank you for this great demonstration. This has been a magnificent pageant. Nothing like it, as General Sherman said. Just think of it! Boston has emptied herself, the country has emptied herself, so to speak, into the streets through which we have passed to-day; and who could see this vast multitude without feeling that there was a revival of the good old spirit of ancient days? When these centennials were first talked of, I thought very little of them; but now I confess I am getting very much in the idea. I believe they will do more than anything else to revive a better spirit. Let us forget the recent past; let us go back to the ancient past, if I may use that expression, and take our lessons from that. Let us look to our ancestors, to the men who founded our institutions, for our examples. In that way, familiarizing ourselves with the history of those times, may we become better men and better citizens, ridding ourselves of the fraud and extravagance which have been the necessary results of the war. We want honesty of purpose; we want the disposition to do, in our own times, if it becomes necessary, as our patriot fathers said they would do, eat no more lamb, if necessary, in order to have more wool to work up into homespun cloth.

I again thank you, and now extend to you a cordial invitation to come down to New Jersey when the proper time arrives.

The President then called for the Governors of Connecticut, New Hampshire and Rhode Island, without obtaining any response. Finally, he called for the Governor of Maine, the representative of a State "which ought to be part of Massachusetts still," and Governor DINGLEY of Maine responded.

REMARKS OF GOVERNOR DINGLEY.

Mr. President, and Fellow-Citizens of the United States: — For standing on ground baptized with the blood of the brave men who, a century since, stood for liberty and nationality, I am sure that we may all take special pride in the fact that we are not so much representatives of individual States as *fellow-citizens* of a common country. You have introduced me, Mr. President, as the representative of that State which was once a part of Massachusetts, and which (as you kindly observed) ought to still occupy that position. I acknowledge the compliment which may be intended in the concession that Maine is worthy of being included in such a grand Commonwealth as Massachusetts; and yet I am sure that after a hundred and thirty years of devoted service in the old homestead, the daughter had reached her majority, and was entitled to set up housekeeping for herself. Assuredly, sir, you can testify that she was a devoted daughter, and did not go forth from the mother's arms until she saw her triumphant over foes abroad and at home, and the acknowledged leader of the best thought and most beneficent ideas of the age. I assure you, sir, that Maine is proud of her political mother, the grand old Commonwealth, and entertains for her an affection which time cannot dim. We feel that the glorious history of the Old Bay State is our history; that her Adams, and Hancock, and Prescott, and Warren belong also to us; and that her battle-fields, her Concord, and Lexington, and Bunker Hill are ours. And, standing to-day on the spot where the martyrs of liberty fell a hundred years ago this very afternoon, I pledge to you, and to the citizens of every other State of our common country here assembled, that the men of Maine will be ready in the future, as they have in the past, to stand shoulder to shoulder with you in defence of the nation which was then made possible. And may this centennial anniversary, and the centennial anniversaries to come, recalling as they do the memories of common sacrifices and common victories, serve to soften the resentments, and strengthen the ties of North and South, and lead the citizens of every section of the republic to acknowledge the stars and stripes as their flag, and the Union, dedicated to freedom and equal rights, as their country and their home.

The Chief Marshal called for "three cheers for Gov. Dingley," which were given with great heartiness.

The President said : — "I stated to the audience that I would call upon our fellow-citizens of the United States in the order of the distance from which they came. We are now at home again, and at home in the United States of America, and I now call upon Vice-President WILSON."

The Vice-President was greeted with three hearty cheers. He spoke as follows : —

REMARKS OF HON. HENRY WILSON.

I am sure, Mr. President, you have not presented me to this vast assemblage at this hour, to weary the ear with speech. Nor have you called me up to be looked at, for there are far better-looking gentlemen around you; besides, it is quite too dark to get a good sight at any one of us. I am here, too, in my own Middlesex. [A voice, "Suffolk now."] Charlestown has escaped from us into Suffolk, but we people of old Middlesex will hold on to Concord, Lexington and Bunker Hill forever more.

I am glad, Mr. President, that we have witnessed this magnificent spectacle. General Sherman tells us, strangers tell us, we know it, for our own eyes have seen it, that this is the grandest demonstration ever beheld upon the North American continent. I hope, I believe too, that this anniversary celebration, the memories associated with this day, the generous spirit that animates all bosoms, will largely contribute to the cause of unity and liberty in the century upon which we have entered. These celebrations at Concord, Lexington and Bunker Hill, like the events they commemorate, tend to inspire all American hearts with patriotism and affectionate regard for our countrymen. I hail this anniversary, I hail the anniversaries upon which we have entered, as grand events, calculated to reunite, reinspire, and reinvigorate the American people, and bind us together with hooks of steel. The Centennial Celebration of the anniversary of Independence is to be in Philadelphia next year. I hope that this anniversary festival will tend to inspire the nation, and that the country and the people of the country will make that the grandest occasion ever witnessed by mortal man. Grand as were the words of Daniel Webster, when the foundations of that Monument were laid, in the presence of Lafayette and the aged heroes of the Revolution; grand as were his words when that Monument had been completed, no words uttered by him were better calculated to do more good, in all this broad land, than are the words uttered here to-day, in the present condition of the country. Let us, sir, all remember that union now, nationality now, development now, are all in harmony with the great, grand, central idea of humanity, the liberties, equal and impartial liberties, of all the children of men.

The President remarked: — "We have received two despatches to-day, one from San Francisco and one from New Orleans. I will ask the Marshal to read them, and then to read a short ode which has been selected from very many contributions offered."

The Marshal read the despatches as follows: —

SAN FRANCISCO, June 17, 1875.

To the HON. GEORGE WASHINGTON WARREN, *President of the Bunker Hill Monument Association:* —

San Francisco, — from the golden gates of the Pacific to the Bunker Hill Association: The citizens of our Western shore send their fraternal greetings to our brethren of the Atlantic coast assembled on Bunker Hill to commemorate the centennial of the great battle fought there. We have our mass meeting to-night.

NEW ORLEANS, June 17, 1875.

GOVERNOR GASTON, *Boston:* —

For myself, and the good people of the Crescent City, I send you greetings from Old Chalmette to Bunker Hill, on the occasion of your Centennial celebration.

JOHN G. PARKER,
Postmaster of New Orleans.

The Marshal then read the following ode, written by GEORGE SENNOTT, Esquire:—

I.

Heroes of Greek Renown!
Ye, who with floods of Persian gore
Purpled Cychreia's sounding shore!
Strong wielders of the Dorian spear—
And ye — dear children of the Dear—
   The Holy Violet Crown!
Ye live to-day. Distance and Time
Vanish before our longing eyes—
And fresh in their eternal prime
   The Demi-Gods arise.

II.

Fierce breed of iron Rome!
Ye whose relentless eagle's wings
O'ershadowing subjugated Kings,
With Death and black Destruction fraught,
To ev'ry hateful Tyrant brought
   His own curs'd lesson home!
Smile sternly now; a free-born race
Here draw your proudest maxims in,
And eagerly, in ampler space,
   And mightier Rome begin!

III.

Savage, yet dauntless crew!
Who broke with grim, unflinching zeal,
The mighty Spaniard's heart of steel,
When ye, with patriotic hands,
Bursting the dykes that kept your lands,
   Let Death and Freedom through!
Arise in glory! Angry floods
And haughty bigots all are tame,
But ye, like liberating gods,
   Have everlasting fame.

IV.

Ye few rock-nurtured Men,
Suliote or Swiss, whose crags defied
Burgundian power and Turkish pride!
Whose deeds, so dear to Freedmen still,
Make every Alp a holy hill —
    A shrine each Suliote glen!
Rejoice to-day! No little bands
Front here th' exulting Tyrant's horde;
But Freedom sways with giant hands
    Her ocean-sweeping sword!

V.

Chiefs of our own blest land,
To whom th' oppressed of all mankind
A sacred refuge look to find!
Of every race the pride and boast,
From wild Atlantic's stormy coast
    To far Pacific's strand!
Millions on millions here maintain
Your generous aims with steady will,
And make our vast imperial reign
    The world's asylum still!

The concluding hymn was then sung by the Apollo Club: —

HYMN.

WORDS BY G. WASHINGTON WARREN — MUSIC BY ABT.

From the blood that steeped this ground,
From the flames which swept around,
Comes to us the grateful sound,
    PLACID PEACE WITH LIBERTY.

Not as now, in plenteous days,
Earned our sires the Patriot's praise,
But by hard and stormy ways,
    Got they us the victory.

Sweet it is to die for thee,
Country fair — now grandly free;
Though to few that lot may be,
   ALL may nobly live for thee.

God who led'st our Fathers forth,
Gav'st our land her second birth,
Bless these States with manly worth,
   Keep them close in harmony.

A benediction was pronounced by the Rev. PHILLIPS BROOKS, and at eight o'clock the exercises at the pavilion were brought to a close.

The following letter has been received from His Excellency Governor INGERSOLL, in response to the call made upon him : —

STATE OF CONNECTICUT.
EXECUTIVE DEPARTMENT,
NEW HAVEN, June 18th, 1875.

DEAR SIR : — I very much regret that, under the erroneous supposition that the exercises at Bunker Hill yesterday would, by reason of the lateness of the hour, close with the oration of General Devens, I left the tent at that time to fulfil another engagement and, therefore, was not present to acknowledge the honor paid to my State by your call upon me among the other guests of the occasion.

It is the singular fortune of Connecticut that, although she sent into the armies of the Revolution more soldiers than any other colony save one, — maintaining in actual service, at one time, out of the State, twenty-two full regiments, when her population but little exceeded two hundred thousand persons, — she must, nevertheless, look beyond her borders for the battle-fields that have been made historic by the valor and the blood of her children. Conspicuous among them all, and by far closer than any by its associations of peculiar force, is that field upon the Charlestown heights, where New England for the first time confronted Old England in war. It was there that our young militia received its "baptism of fire," and our peaceful vines were first emblazoned upon a flag of battle; and it is through the smoke and dust of the conflict around Bunker's Hill that there looms up most distinctly to Connecticut eyes one heroic figure of the Revolution, — the man " who dared to lead where any dared to follow," — Israel Putnam.

It is for these reasons, especially, that it gave me great pleasure to participate in the superb demonstration in Boston yesterday, and that I now regret the circumstances which deprived me of the pleasure of sharing in all the subsequent exercises in Charlestown.

I am, sir, very respectfully yours,

CHARLES R. INGERSOLL.

G. WASHINGTON WARREN, Esq.,
President Bunker Hill Association, etc., etc.,
Charlestown, Mass.

The following letters and despatches were received by the Mayor: —

STATE OF LOUISIANA.
MAYORALTY OF NEW ORLEANS,
CITY HALL, 22d day of May, 1875.

HON. SAMUEL C. COBB, *Mayor of Boston, Mass.:* —

DEAR SIR, — Your esteemed favor of the 17th inst., inviting me to participate in the celebration of the Centennial Anniversary of the Battle of Bunker Hill, and tendering to me the hospitalities of your city, has just been received.

Please return my sincere thanks to the gentlemen of your City Council for their very kind invitation, and say to them that my official duties preclude the possibility of my accepting the same.

Permit me to assure you, sir, that it is with great regret that I have to deny myself the pleasure of visiting your noble city, and of joining with you in the celebration of an event so replete with interest to all true lovers of our country. With my best wishes for your success, and the hope that you will have a glorious celebration, I have the honor to be, sir, with great respect,

        Your obedient servant,
            CHARLES J. LEEDS, *Mayor.*

        CITY OF MEMPHIS.
          MAYOR'S OFFICE,
            MEMPHIS, TENN., May 29th, 1875.
To HIS HONOR SAMUEL C. COBB, *Mayor of Boston, Mass. :* —

DEAR SIR, — Your valued favor of the 17th inst., with invitation, from the committee appointed by the City Council of Boston, to be present at the Centennial Anniversary of the Battle of Bunker Hill, and tendering the hospitalities of the city on the occasion, came duly to hand, for which please accept my sincere and grateful acknowledgments. I postponed answering until now with the hope that it would be possible for me to be present and participate in one of the grandest celebrations which has ever occurred in America. But I am, sir, I regret to say, compelled by a pressure of public business to decline your cordial invitation ; this I regret the more, as the occasion would have afforded me an excellent, and much desired, opportunity to express to you, personally, the thanks of our citizens to the good people of Boston for their liberality and very great kindness to us in the days of affliction gone by.

Americans have, in every section of this vast country, scenes to picture and events to speak of to stimulate national pride ; but nothing will live longer in history than the recollection of the valor and daring of the Minute Men at Bunker Hill ; and none know better how to keep alive a spirit of patriotism and celebrate great events than the people of Massachusetts. May its future be as prosperous as its past has been glorious.

      With assurances of respect,
        I am, dear sir, your obedient servant,
            JOHN LOAGUE, *Mayor.*

CITY OF OMAHA.

To HIS HONOR SAMUEL C. COBB, *Mayor of Boston:* —

DEAR SIR, — I have the honor to acknowledge the receipt of yours of the 17th ult., informing me that the committee appointed by the City Council of Boston, to make arrangements for the celebration of the Centennial Anniversary of the Battle of Bunker Hill, on the 17th of June, 1875, cordially invites me, as Mayor of the City of Omaha, to accept the hospitalities of your city on that occasion.

Since its receipt I have been endeavoring so to arrange my official duties and professional engagements as to accept your most courteous invitation. I find myself, however, at this late day, unable so to do, and am therefore most reluctantly compelled to decline it.

The thought that I might be permitted to be with you and witness the patriotic pageant of that — the great occasion to your city of the present century — has afforded me as much pleasure as the anticipation of being at Philadelphia on the 4th of July, 1876.

Having been raised on a farm in the Old Granite State, one hundred miles from Boston, that city, was, during my early boyhood, before railroads, forty years ago, our chief market. Thence, each winter, as soon as the sleighing permitted, my father — who, allow me to mention here, was born in the same town, Cornish, *on the 4th of July*, 1776 — took his produce to exchange for family supplies.

It was the highest ambition of the boys of my time to visit Boston, and the few who had that privilege were envied by all the others in the neighborhood. It is now thirty years since I have seen your city, but my early attachment to it, and admiration for it, have never ceased. It is indeed a solid city, and worthy of the good name it bears for intelligence and commercial greatness.

In behalf of our young city, which I know has many strong friends in Boston, I thank you and the City Council of your city for this courtesy extended to Omaha, and assure you that the sons of New England, of whom there are many here, will take a deep interest in the celebration which marks the one hundredth anniversary of the Battle of Bunker Hill, — a battle in which the forefathers of some of them participated.

Allow me in closing to offer the following sentiment : —

Bunker Hill Monument and the City of Boston: the one perpetuates the patriotism of worthy sires; the other illustrates the enterprise of dutiful sons.

I am, sir, most respectfully yours,

C. J. CHASE.

MAYOR'S OFFICE, OMAHA, June 5th, 1875.

ALLENTOWN, PA., June 17th, 1875.

To the MAYOR OF BOSTON: —

We are celebrating the battle of Bunker Hill here, to-day, under the auspices of the Ladies' Centennial Association of this city and county. Twenty thousand people are present on the fair grounds participating in the celebration, and witnessing the reproduction by our military of the thrilling scenes of that memorable event. We congratulate you on the procession at Bunker Hill; but Pennsylvania claims as her right a share and interest in the great issues which that struggle helped to inaugurate.

LADIES' CENTENNIAL COMMITTEE.

PHILADELPHIA, June 17th, 1875.

To HIS HONOR THE MAYOR OF BOSTON: —

The National Board of Trade, in session at Philadelphia, pauses, in its consideration of questions relating to the commercial and industrial interests of our common country, and begs to offer to Boston, to Massachusetts, and to the nation at large, its expression of patriotic fervor, its love and devotion to the national life, and its earnest hope that those liberties which the blood of Bunker Hill helped to establish may never be abridged.

By unanimous vote of the board.

FREDERICK FRALEY, *President.*
CHARLES RANDOLPH, *Secretary.*

APPENDIX.

THE LITERATURE OF BUNKER HILL,

WITH ITS ANTECEDENTS AND RESULTS.

[PREPARED BY JUSTIN WINSOR, SUPERINTENDENT OF THE BOSTON PUBLIC LIBRARY.]

[NOTE. — The following survey of the literature of the history of Boston during the Revolutionary period, beginning with the excitement over the application for "Writs of Assistance" in 1761, and ending with the transfer of the seat of actual war, upon the evacuation of Boston, in March, 1776, — has been prepared to meet the renewed interest incident to the centennial celebrations. It is not intended to make reference to all works, but only to such as are indicative in some respect.]

WRITS OF ASSISTANCE, 1761.

Shortly after the close of the French war, when the British government was no longer dependent on the friendly assistance of the colonies, and revenue was to be got from enforcing the acts of trade, the application of the agents of government for "Writs of Assistance" was met by James Otis in his plea against the grant. Tudor's life of Otis makes that patriot the centre of interest at this period, and the legal aspects of the case can be studied in Horace Gray's Appendix to the Reports of cases in the Superior Court, 1761-1772, by Josiah Quincy. The third volume of Hutchinson's "History of Massachusetts," 1750-1774, gives the governmental view, while in Minot's History, 1748-1765, the patriot side is sustained, and this view is represented in the lives of Josiah Quincy, John Adams, and Samuel Adams. In its broad relations as indicating the temper of the people it is discussed by Bancroft in his "History of the United States;" by Hildreth in his "History of the United States;" by Frothingham in his "Rise of the Republic;" by Barry, in his "History of Massachusetts," etc.

APPENDIX.

STAMP ACT, 1765.

To the authorities named in the preceding section may be added, for local coloring, the chapters in the histories of Boston by Drake, and by Snow. See also ch. 14 of Tudor's Otis.

1767-1775.

This period and its patriotic movements are made the special theme of Frothingham's "Warren and his Times;" and in the same author's "Rise of the Republic" the action of the patriots is viewed as tending to form the national spirit. A chapter in Tudor's Otis is given to characterizing the people of Boston at this time; and in the collection of contemporary documents called Niles's "Principles and Acts of the Revolution," the spirit of the people can be read in their own words and writings. In Mercy Warren's (she was a sister of James Otis) "History of the American Revolution" we have the characters of the most distinguished of the patriots drawn by one who knew them closely.

The influence of the press is traced in the third era of Hudson's "History of American Journalism," and the aspects can be studied in the files of the five newspapers published in Boston at this time: —

Fleet's Evening Post, patronized both by the whigs and the government.

The Boston Newsletter, the only paper which continued to be published during the siege.

The Massachusetts Gazette, the chief organ of the government.

The Boston Gazette, devoted to the patriots.

The Massachusetts Spy, devoted to the patriots.

The most important journal out of Boston was the Essex Gazette.

For the influence of the clergy, see Thornton's "Pulpit of the Revolution," and the "Patriot Preachers of the Revolution," 1860.

As before, the lives of leading patriots must be consulted, —Wells's "Life of Samuel Adams;" the life and diaries of John Adams; Quincy's "Life of Josiah Quincy;" Austin's "Life of Elbridge Gerry;" and the general histories, like those of the United States by Bancroft and Hildreth; and those of Massachusetts by Minot and Barry, etc.

The third volume of Hutchinson's Massachusetts still gives the tory view, and the later British estimate of the period is found in Mahon's (Stanhope's) "History of England."

For the local associations of the Province House, Green Dragon Tavern, etc., see Shurtleff's "Description of Boston," and Drake's "Old Landmarks and Historic Personages of Boston."

BOSTON MASSACRE, 1770.

Frothingham, in his articles in the Atlantic Monthly, June and August, 1862, and November, 1863, on the "Sam Adams Regiments," traces carefully the progress of events from October, 1768, which culminated in the massacre in March, 1770, and this matter is epitomized in ch. 6 of his "Life of Warren." Bancroft treats it in all its relations, in chapter 43 of his sixth volume; and it is the subject of special treatment by Kidder in his "Boston Massacre," and in the introduction to Loring's "Hundred Boston Orators." Capt. Preston, the royal officer who commanded the soldiers, was defended at his trial by John Adams and Josiah Quincy, and the lives of these patriots treat of their defence. The accounts of the trial, and the collection of orations delivered on succeeding anniversaries, are necessary to a full understanding of the event.

See also Snow's "History of Boston," the lives of Otis, Samuel Adams, etc., and the general histories.

Crispus Attucks, one of the slain, usually called a mulatto, is held to have been a half-breed Indian in the American Historical Record, Dec., 1872.

THE TEA PARTY, DEC., 1773.

Frothingham, in his "Life of Warren," ch. 9, has given the details, and in his "Rise of the Republic," ch. 8, has shown its political significance, and has again taken a general survey in his Centennial paper, in the Proceedings of the Massachusetts Historical Society, Dec., 1873. See also the collections of this Society, 4th series, vol. III. In ch. 2 of Reed's "Life of Joseph Reed," and in Sparks's "Washington," the relations of the patriots of Boston to those of the other colonies at this time can be studied. Bancroft gives to it ch. 50 of his sixth volume; and Barry, ch. 15 of his second volume. Hewes, an actor in the scenes, has given an account in his "Traits of the Tea Party." There are illustrative documents in Force's "American Archives," vol. I.; in Niles's "Principles and Acts of the Revolution;" and the contemporary accounts and records have been reprinted from the Boston Gazette of Dec. 6, 1773, by Poole, in one of the State Registers.

See further Tudor's "Life of Otis," ch. 21; Snow's "Boston;" Niles's Register, 1827, vol. XXXIII., p. 75, from Flint's Western Monthly Review for July, 1827; Lossing in Harper's Monthly, vol. IV.

BOSTON PORT BILL, 1774.

General Gage arrived in Boston in May, to put the provisions of this bill in force, June 12. Its political bearings can be traced in Bancroft, and in Frothingham's Warren, ch. 10, and in his "Rise of the Republic;" and the military sequel in Frothingham's "Siege of Boston." See also Tudor's Otis; Wells's Samuel Adams; "Life of John Adams;" "Life of Josiah Quincy."

Illustrative documents will be found in Force, vol. II. See the diary of Thomas Newell, in Boston, Nov., 1773, to Dec., 1774, in Proceedings of Massachusetts Historical Society, Feb., 1859, and in their Collections, 4th series, vol. I. The Correspondence of the Boston Donation Committee, relative to the supplies sent to the embargoed town from other places, is given in the Massachusetts Historical Society's Collections, 4th series, vol. IV. For correspondence of the Boston patriots with those of the other colonies, see Reed's "Life of Joseph Reed."

The Suffolk Resolves, passed at Milton, Sept. 9, 1774, can be found in the appendix to Frothingham's Warren.

1775, JANUARY — MARCH.

For the interval before the actual hostilities at Concord, still follow Frothingham's "Siege of Boston," ch. 2, and consult for illustrative documents Force's "American Archives," vol. I., where will be found Berniere's narrative of his explorations towards Worcester, to get information for General Gage. For particulars of Leslie's expedition to Salem, in March, see Endicott's article in the Proceedings of the Essex Institute, vol. 1.; and the "Life of Timothy Pickering," vol. 1. Also, George B. Loring's, and other addresses at the Centennial Celebration, 1875. The contemporary evidence relative to the expedition to Marshfield can be found in Force's "American Archives."

E. E. Hale's popular summary, "One Hundred Years Ago," begins with these preliminaries of war.

1775, APRIL, LEXINGTON AND CONCORD.

The best eclectic account is that in Frothingham's "Siege of Boston," and in his appendix will be found a chronological list of the principal authorities.

Paul Revere's expedition on the night of the 18th, to give notice of the morrow's march, which is the subject of Longfellow's poem, was narrated by himself, and appears in the Collections of the Massachusetts Historical Society, first series, vol. v. See, in this connection, on the escape of Hancock and Adams, Loring's "Hundred Boston Orators," and General Sumner in the New England Historical and Genealogical Register, VIII., p. 188.

The narrative and depositions ordered by the Provincial Congress were printed in the "Journal of the Third Provincial Congress, 1775;" in the London Chronicle, and in various Boston newspapers, and the whole reappeared in a pamphlet, issued by Isaiah Thomas, and entitled "A Narrative of the Incursions and Ravages of the King's Troops on the Nineteenth of April," and is given in Force's "American Archives." This matter constituted the account sent by the Congress to England, with the Essex Gazette, which was the chief newspaper narrative, and which reached London eleven days ahead of General Gage's messenger, and, in this connection, see the Proceedings of the Massachusetts Historical Society, April, 1858. Other accounts and depositions, as well as those transmitted to the Continental Congress, can also be found in Force's "American Archives;" in Frothingham's "Siege of Boston;" in Shattuck's "History of Concord;" in Dawson's "Battles of the United States;" in Frank Moore's "Diary of the Revolution," etc. The Rev. Wm. Gordon, May 17, 1775, prepared "An Account of the Commencement of Hostilities," which is reprinted in Force, and this, with additions and abridgments, forms part of his "History of the Revolution."

The Rev. Jonas Clark delivered a discourse in Lexington on the first anniversary in 1776, and appended to it a narrative of events which has been reprinted in 1875 in large quarto. A brief account was also prepared by the Rev. Wm. Emerson, of Concord, a witness of the events at Concord, and this was printed in R. W. Emerson's centennial discourse in 1835.

Of the British accounts, Col. Smith's report will be found in the Appendix to Mahon's (Stanhope's) England. Various English accounts are given in Force, and in "The Detail and Conduct of the American War." General Gage sent to Governor Trumbull a "Circumstantial Account," which is printed in the Massachusetts Historical Society's Collections, second series, vol. II., while in vol. IV. will be found a reprint of a pamphlet originally printed in 1779, from a manuscript left in Boston by a British officer, which gives Gage's instructions to Brown and De Berniere, Feb. 22, 1775, with an account of their journey to Worcester and Concord, and a narrative of the "Transactions" on the 19th of April. Stedman's "History of the American War," and the other British writers claim that the provincials fired first at Lexington; and Pitcairn's side of the story is given from Stiles's diary in Frothingham, and in Irving's "Washington," etc.

Late in the day General Heath exercised a general command over the provincials, and his Memoirs can be consulted. Col. Timothy Pickering's Essex Regiment was charged with dilatoriness in coming up, and this question is discussed in the "Life of Pickering," ch. 5 of vol. I.

The semi-centennial period renewed the interest in the matter, and the question, whether the provincials returned the fire of the British troops at Lexington, was discussed with some spirit. This having been denied, a committee of the town of Lexington authorized Elias Phinney to publish an account of "The Battle of Lexington," to which were appended depositions (taken in 1822) of survivors to establish the point. This led the Rev. Ezra Ripley and others, of Concord, in 1827, to publish "The Fight at Concord," claiming the credit of first returning the fire for Concord, and this was reissued in 1832. In 1835 the story was again told in the interest of Concord, in

Lemuel Shattuck's "History of Concord," which was reviewed in the North American Review, vol. XLII. In this account, as well as that by Ripley and others, it was claimed that the part borne by Captain Davis, of Acton was not fairly represented, and Josiah Adams, in his centennial address at Acton, in 1835, and again in a letter to Shattuck in 1850, presented the merits of Davis, and gave depositions of survivors. The parts borne by other towns have also been commemorated, for Danvers, by D. P. King, in 1835; for Cambridge, by Mackenzie, in 1870; and also see S. A. Smith's " West Cambridge on the 19th of April, 1775."

At Lexington, Edward Everett delivered an address in 1835, but see also his Mount Vernon Papers, No. 47; and there is an account of the celebration in Niles's Register, vol. XLVIII., and a plan of the Lexington field can be found in Josiah Adams's letter, and in Moore's " Ballad History of the Revolution," No. 1. See also Hudson's " History of Lexington," ch. 6, and a popular narrative in Harper's Monthly, vol. XX., and accounts in association with landmarks in Lossing's " Field-book," and in Drake's " Historic Fields and Mansions of Middlesex." See also R. H. Dana's address in 1875, and the centennial " Souvenir of 1775."

At Concord, Edward Everett delivered an address in 1825, and much of interest in connection with this anniversary was printed in the newspapers of that day, and Lossing and Drake should also be consulted for much illustrative of the events of 1775. Popular narratives can be found in Frederic Hudson's illustrated paper in Harper's Monthly, May, 1875, and in the article by G. Reynolds in the Unitarian Review for April, 1875. See also George W. Curtis's oration in 1875, and James R. Lowell's ode, in Atlantic Monthly, June, 1875. Also the Rev. Henry Westcott's Centennial Sermons, 1875.

The events of the 19th of April also form important chapters in Bancroft's " United States;" in Elliott's " New England;" in Barry's "Massachusetts," and in other general works on the revolutionary period. Also see Dawson's " Battles of the United States;" E. E. Hale's " One Hundred Years Ago;" and Potter's American Monthly, April, 1875.

Amos Doolittle's contemporary engravings of the events are reproduced in a new edition of Clark's narrative. See, also, Moore's

"Ballad History," part 1; and Potter's American Monthly, April, 1875. There is a view of Concord taken in 1776, in the Massachusetts Magazine, July, 1794.

An account of Jonathan Harrington, the last survivor of the fight, is given in Potter's American Monthly, July, 1875. See also Lossing's "Field-book of the Revolution."

Claims have been raised for other places as having been the first to shed blood in the war, for which see the Historical Magazine, Jan., 1869, and Potter's American Monthly, April, 1875.

The events of the interval between Concord and Bunker Hill can best be studied in Frothingham's "Siege of Boston." Particularly on the affair at Noddle's Island, May 27, 1775, see Force's "American Archives," Humphrey's "Life of Putnam," and a chapter in Dawson's "Battles of the United States."

1775, JUNE 17, BUNKER HILL.

Frothingham, in an appendix to his "Siege of Boston," enumerates in chronological order the chief authoritative statements regarding the battle. Dawson devoted the whole of the June, 1868, double number of the Historical Magazine to a collation of nearly all the printed accounts, authoritative and compiled, and from his foot-notes can be gleaned a full list of articles and books which at that time had been published.

The affairs of the 19th of April had among other results precipitated the removal of the newspapers published in Boston to other places, and the number for April 24 was the last of the Evening Post published in Boston. Edes's Boston Gazette, which was thus removed to Watertown, the seat of the Provincial Congress, gave, in its issue for June 19, the earliest account of the battle which appeared in print. The Massachusetts Spy, which had been removed to Worcester in May, had its first account in its number for June 21. That same day the Connecticut Journal had its first intelligence, and though it was several days later before the New York papers published accounts, on this same 21st a handbill with the news was circulated in New York. In F. Moore's "Diary of the American Revolution," there will be found a list of the contemporary newspapers publishing these accounts, and from which he derives in part the matter of his book, which begins Jan. 1, 1775. Many of these accounts will be found reprinted in Dawson's Historical Magazine article; and some of them have been reproduced in *fac-simile* in the centennial memorials of the present year. Frothingham reprints that of the Massachusetts Spy in his recent condensed narrative of the battle, and it is in *fac-simile* in the "Centennial Graphic." Almon's Remembrancer, London, was begun June 15, 1775, for gathering from English and American sources the fugitive and contemporary accounts.

The Rev. Mr. Thacher was a spectator of the action, from the north side of the Mystic river, and within a fortnight afterwards, and depending in some measure upon Prescott's assistance, prepared an account, the manuscript of which is now preserved in the American Antiquarian Society's collection at Worcester. This had been used by Frothingham and others, but was never printed in full with all its corrections indicated, till Dawson included it in his appendix in 1868. This narrative of Thacher's was made the basis of that which the Committee of Safety prepared for transmission to England, and this latter narrative is given with much other matter in "The Journal of the Third Provincial Congress, 1775," and has been reprinted by Ellis (in 1843), Frothingham, Swett, Dawson, etc. Force's "American Archives," vol. IV., is another repository of these and various other contemporary accounts, several of which are copied by Dawson in his "Battles of the United States," as well as in his Historical Magazine article; and by F. Moore in his "Ballad History of the American Revolution," part 2. Colonel Prescott's own account is contained in a letter dated August 25, 1775, and addressed to John Adams, and this can be seen in Frothingham, where it was first published, and in Dawson. What is called the "Prescott MS.," which is said to have been prepared in the family of the colonel, and in part with his approval, was first printed in full in Butler's "History of Groton," p. 337, etc., and it has been reprinted by Dawson, p. 437. Frothingham and Sparks had the use of the manuscript known as Judge Prescott's (son of the colonel) memoir of the battle; but it has never been printed in full. Contemporary feelings will be found expressed in Mrs. Adams's letters.

President Stiles, then of Newport, kept a diary of events at this time, which is preserved at Yale College. He first heard the news on the 18th, and began his account on that day, to which he added from day to day, as further corrected tidings reached him. This was printed at length for the first time in Dawson, but has been used by Sparks, Frothingham, Bancroft, etc. This diary also copies the letter of Peter Brown, dated June 25, to his mother, which is considered by Frothingham, who gives it, as the most noteworthy description written by a private soldier engaged in the battle, and is printed from the original in Potter's American Monthly, July, 1875. Col. Scammons's account of his court martial is given in the New England Chronicle, Feb. 29, 1776, and is reprinted in Dawson, p. 400. Governor Trumbull, in a letter, August 31, 1779, gave a sketch of the action, and it is printed in the Massachusetts Historical Society's Collections, vol. vi. Col. John Trumbull, who afterwards painted the well-known picture of the battle, was not in it, but saw the smoke of it from the Roxbury lines, and in his autobiography, published in 1841, has an outline narrative. General Heath's memoirs, published in 1798, have a brief account. The narrative in Thacher's military journal is entered as having been written in July, 1775. The memoirs of General James Wilkinson, printed in 1816 give, in ch. 19, a "rapid sketch," embodying his own knowledge and other evidence which had reached him at first hand, as he went over the field in March, 1776, with Stark and Reed, and conferred with Major Caleb Stark.

Other testimony of eye-witnesses was gathered too long after the battle to be wholly trustworthy, in 1818, at the time of the Dearborn controversy, later to be mentioned, and numerous depositions were taken from survivors attending the semi-centennial celebration, which are preserved in three large volumes, but are considered by those who have examined them as of little or no value. There is a long account in the Columbian Centinel of December, 1824, and January, 1825. An account by Oliver Morsman, "a revolutionary soldier," was published at Sacket's Harbor, in 1830. Mr. Needham Maynard contributed the recollections of a survivor, which were printed in a Boston newspaper as late as 1843.

Of the British accounts, the entries in Howe's orderly book are given in Ellis's sketch, 1843 edition. The Gentleman's Magazine of the same year (London) gave an account, with a somewhat erroneous plan of the redoubt, which has been reproduced in Frothingham's monographs. General Gage's official report was printed in Almon's "Remembrancer," accompanied with strictures upon it, and it has been reprinted by Ellis (1843 ed. with the strictures), Force, Swett, Frothingham; by Dawson, in his Historical Magazine and in his "Battles;" in Frank Moore's "Ballad History," etc. Burgoyne saw the action from Copp's Hill, and his letter to Lord Stanley, dated June 25, 1775, has also been given in Dawson; in Ellis's ed. of 1843; in the New England Historical and Genealogical Register, April, 1857; in an appendix in Pulsifer's sketch of the battle, issued two or three years since, and is also given in S. A. Drake's "Bunker Hill; the story told in Letters from the Battlefield;" in which also will be found, together with various other minor British accounts, the "Impartial and Authentic Narration," originally published at London, 1775, by John Clarke, "a first lieutenant of marines," who gives what purports to be a speech of Howe to his troops previous to the advance, which, with much else in this somewhat extended narrative, is considered rather apocryphal. The compiled account in the Annual Register has been thought to have been written by Burke. Force, Ellis's ed. of 1843, and Dawson, gather various of the contemporary royalist accounts, and some particulars can be found in the separate historic records detailing the careers of some of the royal regiments in the action, like the Fourth, Fifth, Tenth Foot, etc. Moorsom's Fifty-second regiment gives a brief account of its share in the battle, with plates of their uniform at the time. See also Sergeant Lamb's (Welsh Fusileers) "Journal of Occurrences during the late American War;" and the "Detail and Conduct of the American War," for a letter from Boston, July 5, 1775, and other British accounts. The British accounts first took regular shape in Stedman's "History of the American War," published in 1794. Howe's conduct of the battle is criticised in Lee's "Memoirs of the War in the Southern Department." Mahon's (Stanhope) "History of England" represents in his account, otherwise fair, that the Americans then, and since, have considered the battle a victory; but when called upon to substantiate such an assertion relied chiefly (see his appendix) on the reports of British tourists of a subsequent day.

In 1858, Mr. Henry B. Dawson published a popular account of the "Battles of the United States," giving a chapter, based on the ordinary authorities, to Bunker Hill. In 1868, in the Historical Magazine, an American periodical, then edited by him, he gave a special study of the battle, in which the "colonists" of the earlier work became "insurgents," and the royal troops were represented as fighting "in support of the constitution, the laws, the king and the government, and in defence of the life of the nation." Differing from other authorities, he represents that the attack along the beach of the Mystic was a preliminary attack. He has elaborately collated the various contemporary and later compiled accounts, and has appended numerous illustrative documents by English and American writers, derived from Almon, Force, Ellis, Frothingham, and others, to which he adds several printed for the first time. The fac-similes of Page's, De Berniere's and Dearborn's maps, which are mentioned in his text as given with his account, were never appended to it.

Of the more extended descriptions, that in Frothingham's "Siege of Boston" is distinctively marked for its dependence chiefly upon contemporary accounts, and its avoidance of the mingled recollections and self-deceptions of the survivors of all grades, who, in 1818, furnished so many depositions, over forty years after the conflict, to perplex the truth-lover. These confused recollections, added to the local jealousies of the partisans of the troops of Massachusetts, New Hampshire and Connecticut, and to the facts narrated by different persons as having taken place in positions so disconnected as the redoubt and the rail-fence, have done much to render the sifting of evidence very necessary; and it all gave some ground for Charles Hudson, in 1857, in his "Doubts concerning the Battle of Bunker Hill" [see also Christian Examiner, vol. XL.], to attempt a logical venture somewhat after the fashion of Whateley's famous argument on the non-existence of Napoleon. When, later, Frothingham wrote the "Life of Joseph Warren," he took occasion to summarize his longer narrative in a chapter of that book, and his whole description has again been recast in a popular form in his recent centennial "Bunker Hill," where he has added much new matter, in letters, incidents, etc.

Anniversary addresses have often rehearsed the story, occasionally adding a few details to our stock of information, and the most significant among them have been Webster's, in 1825 [see also Analectic Magazine, vol. XI.], at the laying of the corner-stone of the Monument; Alexander H. Everett's, in 1836, which subsequently was inwoven in his life of Warren, in Sparks's series; the Rev. Dr. Geo. E. Ellis's, in 1841, which was subsequently issued in 1843, anonymously, as a sketch of the battle, with an appendix of illustrative documents, some of which were printed for the first time, and has again, in 1875, been recast in a centennial history without the illustrative documents; but see also his account in the New York Herald, June 8, 1875; that by Edward Everett, and that by Judge Devens in 1875. A succinct narrative of the battle was also once or twice printed by Alden Bradford, in connection with his studies in the history of Massachusetts. A recent "New History of the Battle," by W. W. Wheildon, traces two separate engagements constituting the battle. The last two or three years have produced condensed summaries, like that of Pulsifer, and S. A. Drake's; that by James M. Bugbee, in Osgood's Centennial Memorial; an article by H. E. Scudder, in the Atlantic Monthly, July, 1875; one by Launce Poyntz, in the Galaxy, July, 1875. It also makes ch. 4 of E. E. Hale's "One Hundred Years Ago," and the story is retold in the Centennial numbers of Frank Leslie's Pictorial, in the "Centennial Graphic," and in various other popular memorials of 1875. The story is also told discursively in the illustrated paper, by Rev. Dr. Samuel Osgood, in the July (1875) number of Harper's Monthly; and with particular reference to landmarks, in Lossing's "Field-book of the Revolution," vol. I., which account also appeared in the first volume of Harper's Monthly; in S. A. Drake's "Historic Fields and Mansions of Middlesex." Finch, in an article in Silliman's Journal, 1822, gave an account of the traces then existing of the works of the British and Americans in the siege of Boston, and this has been reprinted by Frothingham.

The battle has necessarily given a subject to chapters in the general histories of the war and of the State. The earliest American historian of the war was Gordon [see Loring on Gordon's History in Historical Magazine, February and March, 1862], and he followed closely the account of the Committee of Safety. Ramsay's "American Revolution" was published in 1789; Mrs. Mercy Warren's, later; Hubley's, in 1805. Bancroft gives to it the 38th chapter of his seventh volume. It is described in ch. 20 of the second volume of Elliott's "New England," and in the third volume of Barry's "Massachusetts." The biographers of Washington, like Marshall and Irving, needed to describe it as leading to the consolidation of the army of which he took command on the 3d of July next following. There is a brief account in Tudor's "Life of Otis." The memoirs of Heath have already been mentioned, and the lives of other observers and participants will give occasional minor details.

For the part borne by *New Hampshire troops*, see the memoirs of Stark, and Edward Everett's "Life of Stark." Stark's report to the New Hampshire congress is in the New Hampshire Historical Society's Collections, vol. II.; in Ellis's ed. of 1843, etc. The adjutant-general of New Hampshire, in his report for 1866, second volume, rehearses the military history of that State, and gives some details regarding the troops of that province which were engaged. The manuscripts in the adjutant-general's office (New Hampshire), containing the rosters of Stark's and Reed's regiments, have never been printed in full. C. C. Coffin, in a letter in the Boston Globe, June 23, 1875, epitomizes the service of New Hampshire troops in the battle; and details will be found in the New Hampshire Provincial Papers, vol. VII.; in the histories of the towns of Hollis, whence came Capt. Dow's company of Prescott's regiment; of Manchester, by Potter, whence came Capt. John Moore's company of Stark's regiment; and of New Ipswich. See also the New England Historical and Genealogical Register, vol. XXVII., p. 377, etc.

The question of the highest *command in the battle* has given rise to much controversy. In many of the unauthoritative contemporary accounts, particularly in the British ones, Warren is represented as the commander. Putnam is known to have been the adviser of the expedition in the Council of War, and in the less authoritative accounts of the time is represented, as also in engravings, as the responsible director. Gordon, in his history in 1788, was the earliest, in print, to give the command to Prescott, following the Committee of Safety's account. The earliest printed direct mention of Putnam as commander is in a note to the sermon preached at his funeral by Rev. Josiah Whitney, in 1790, where he took exception to Humphrey's statement in his " Life of Putnam," 1788, published while Putnam was still living, in which no mention is made of Putnam having commanded. Eliot, in his " Biographical Dictionary," in 1809, represents Prescott as commanding in the redoubt, and Stark at the rail-fence. The earliest reflection upon the conduct of Putnam in the action appeared in General Wilkinson's memoirs, which were published in 1816, and were reviewed in the North American, October, 1817. The Analectic Magazine for February and March, 1818, had articles on the battle, following chiefly the accounts of Thacher and Gordon, but with some important differences, and giving documents in the latter number.

General Henry Dearborn, who was a captain in Stark's regiment at the rail-fence, opened a controversy, not yet ended, and which at that time soon got to have a political bearing, when he printed his communication in the Portfolio for March, 1818, in which he aimed to show that during the battle Putnam remained inactive at the rear, and this paper has since been reprinted separately; and twice in the Historical Magazine, August, 1864, and June, 1868, p. 402. Colonel Daniel Putnam, the son of the general, replied to Dearborn in the May number of the Portfolio, and appended numerous depositions, all of which have been reprinted in Dawson, p. 407.

This reply of Daniel Putnam led General Dearborn to vindicate his former statement by the publication in the Boston Patriot of June 13, 1818, of various depositions and confirmations of other participants, all of which may also be found in Dawson, p. 414. At this time, Daniel Webster, in the North American Review, July, 1818, vindicated the character of Putnam, but, examining the evidence judicially, came to the conclusion that Prescott commanded the fatigue party during the night, and on the subsequent day exercised a general command over the field so far as he could, and should be considered the commanding officer, and as acting under the orders of

General Ward, at Cambridge, only, and to whom he made report of the action after it was over. See also the Proceedings of the Massachusetts Historical Society for June, 1858.

Judge John Lowell next reviewed Dearborn's defence of his attack on Putnam in the Columbian Centinel for July 4 and 15, 1818, and strengthened his points with counter-depositions of actors in the struggle, all of which is again given in Dawson, p. 423. Colonel Swett now entered into the controversy in an "Historical and Topographical Sketch of Bunker Hill Battle," which, in October, 1818, was appended to an edition of Humphrey's "Life of Putnam," and this sketch was subsequently published separately and with enlargements, derived in part from conversations with the survivors who attended the semi-centennial jubilee of 1825, and this appeared in 1826, and again in 1827; but see Sparks's notice in the North American Review, vol. XXII. Meanwhile, Col. Daniel Putnam, in 1825, recapitulated his views in a communication to the Bunker Hill Monument Association, and this document is printed in the Connecticut Historical Collections, vol. I. The account of Swett has been substantially followed in Rand, Avery & Co.'s "Bunker Hill Centennial." Swett's first publication was criticised by D. L. Child, in the Boston Patriot, November 17, 1818, who claimed that Putnam was not in the battle, and whose article was reprinted as an "Enquiry into the Conduct of General Putnam." On the other hand, Alden Bradford, in his pamphlet, in 1825, claimed the command for Putnam. In 1841, Ellis, in his oration, and subsequently in his "History of the Battle," in 1843, taking advantage of intercourse with Prescott's descendants, made the first extended presentation of Prescott's claims, to which Col. Swett demurred in the Boston Advertiser, where also can be found Ellis's rejoinder. Again, in 1843, John Fellows, in his "Veil Removed," animadverted upon Swett's views regarding Putnam, and reproduced Dearborn's statements and many others aimed to detract from Putnam's fame.

When Frothingham's "Siege of Boston" appeared in 1849, in which the question of the command was critically examined, p. 159, etc., giving that power to Prescott, Swett renewed the controversy in a critique on that work in 1850, with a tract, "Who was the

Commander," etc., to which Frothingham replied in a pamphlet of fifty-six pages, "The Command in the Battle of Bunker Hill," substantiating his position, and pointing out the inconsistencies and seeming perversions of Swett. In 1853, Irving, in his "Life of Washington," favored Prescott. In 1855, L. Grosvenor, in an address before the descendants of General Putnam, "exposed" (as he claimed) "the ungenerous conduct of Colonel Prescott toward General Putnam, *the* commander in the battle." When Bancroft, in 1858, published his seventh volume, he took the ground, already foreshadowed in a lecture which he had delivered, that Prescott commanded the provincials. In 1859, "Selah," of the Hartford Post, favoring Putnam, had a controversy with Dawson, who held Putnam to have been a "blusterer and swaggerer," and intimates he was also treacherous; and this was reprinted in an unpublished quarto, "Major General Israel Putnam." Again, in Putnam's favor, the Hon. H. C. Deming delivered a discourse before the Connecticut Historical Society on the presentation of Putnam's sword, and it was repeated, June 18, 1860, at Putnam's grave, at Pomfret, before the Putnam Phalanx. The argument, as regards the claims of Putnam, was presented by the Rev. I. N. Tarbox, in the New York Herald, June 12 and 14, 1875, and in the New Englander, April, 1875. S. A. Drake's "General Israel Putnam, the Commander at Bunker Hill," argues on the basis of military rule, and summarizes the authorities. See also Hollister's "History of Connecticut," and Hinman's "Connecticut in the Revolution." Judge Devens's oration at Bunker Hill, 1875, favors Prescott. Wheildon's "New History" favors Putnam. A pamphlet, "Col. William Prescott," by Francis J. Parker, issued since the centennial celebration, presents the case anew in favor of that officer.

In 1825, when General W. H. Sumner was adjutant-general of Massachusetts, and it devolved upon him to arrange for the appearance of the veterans in the celebration of that year, he collected from the recitals of some of them some particulars regarding the appearance and death of Warren, and held some correspondence with Dr. Waterhouse on the subject in the Boston Patriot, in August of that year. This matter he reproduced in a paper in the New England Historical and Genealogical Register, April and July, 1858. See further the accounts in Loring's "Hundred Boston Orators;" in Mrs. J. B. Brown's [Warren's grand-daughter] "Stories of General Warren;" in Dr. John Jeffries' [son of the royal surgeon on the field] paper in the Boston Medical and Surgical Journal, June 17, 1875; and in the life of Dr. John Warren, brother of the general. See also the eulogy on General Warren in 1776 by Perez Morton, and the memorial volume issued on the occasion of the dedication of the Warren statue, and particularly Frothingham's "Life of Warren." There is an account of the different celebrations in Charlestown in the New York Herald for June 4, 1875.

There are other papers on the battle in the New England Historical and Genealogical Register, and Dawson's and Frothingham's notes will indicate additional publications not mentioned here.

The earliest of the plans of the action seems to have been a slight sketch, after information from Chaplain John Martin, who was in the battle, drawn by Stiles in his diary, which is reproduced in Dawson, who also, as does Frothingham, gives the slight sketch, made with printers' rules, which accompanied the account in Rivington's Gazette, August 3, 1775.

The careful plan made by Page of the British engineers, based upon Capt. Montresor's survey (which closely agrees with Felton and Parker's survey of Charlestown in 1848), is much the best, and it shows the laying out of Charlestown, the position of the frigates, and the battery at Copp's Hill. The successive positions of the attacking force are indicated by a superposed sheet. This was issued in London in 1776, and the same plate, with few changes, was used in Stedman's history in 1794. The original impression was re-engraved for Frothingham's "Siege," and is also given in his centennial narrative.

The plan by De Berniere of the Tenth Royal Infantry, on much the same scale as Page's, differs in some points from it, is not so correct in the ground plan, and is the first plan that appeared in an American engraving, in the Analectic Magazine, February, 1818, where it is represented as from a sketch found in the captured baggage of a British officer, in 1775. General Dearborn made some remarks on this plan in the Portfolio, March, 1818, which are reprinted in Dawson, p. 438. Dearborn's subsequent plan, as altered in red on that of De Berniere, was criticised upon the field in June, 1818, by Governor Brooks (who acted as messenger from Prescott to Ward in the battle), as detailed by General Sumner in the New England Historical and Genealogical Register, July, 1858. This map was made the basis of one engraved by Smith, and issued in Boston, at the time of the completion of the Monument, in 1843.

A map of Boston, showing Charlestown and the field, with Burgoyne's letter attached, was issued in London, and has been reproduced in fac-simile in F. Moore's "Ballad History of the Revolution," part 2.

There is also an English map of the eastern part of Massachusetts, dated London, September 2d, 1775, in which the lines of march of the troops of the different provinces are designated as they assembled to the relief of Boston. This has been reproduced in smaller size in the "Centennial Graphic," and Frothingham styles it "more curious than valuable." In a side-sketch, of this same sheet, there is a semi-pictorial plan of the battle, with the whole of Boston, and this has recently been fac-similed in Wheildon's, Pulsifer's and Bugbee's sketches, and in George A. Coolidge's "Centennial Memorial."

Colonel Swett made a plan of his own, based on Berniere's, of about the size of Page's, and it was reproduced full size in Ellis's Oration, 1841; but the reproductions of it in Lossing's "Field-book," in Ellis's New York Herald article, June 8, 1875, and in his History and Centennial History, in Rand, Avery & Co.'s "Bunker Hill Centennial," in George A. Coolidge's "Brochure," in the Bunker Hill Times, June 17, 1875, and in Bugbee's sketch, are reduced in size. Little regard is paid in this plan to the laying out of the town of Charlestown. See also the plan in the English translation of Botta's "History of the War of Independence."

Of contemporary plans of Boston, that in the Gentleman's Magazine, October, 1775, p. 464, shows the peninsula, with "Charlestown in ruins." This is drawn from the same original as that in the Pennsylvania Magazine, 1775, which in the June number has a plan of Boston Harbor, with only one eminence delineated on the Charlestown peninsula, which is marked "Bunk' H." The houses in the town are represented as on fire. The London Magazine, April, 1774, has a chart of the coast of New England, with a plan of Boston in the corner, and this plan was inserted, enlarged, in Jeffery's "Map of New England," Nov., 1774, with also a plan of Boston harbor, and was again copied in Jeffery's "American Atlas," 1776, and a French reproduction of it was published at Paris, in 1778, in the "Atlas Ameriquain Septentrional.".

There are rude contemporary views of the action, one of which appeared in 1775, known as Roman's, represents Putnam on horseback, as in command, and was reduced in the Pennsylvania Magazine, September, 1775, and this has been heliotyped in Frothingham's centennial sketch, in Rand, Avery & Co.'s, and in Coolidge's "Memorials," and is also reproduced in Moore's "Ballad History," and in the Bunker Hill Times, June 17, 1875. In Cocking's poem, "The American War," published in London, 1781, is a somewhat extraordinary picture, which, with extracts from the poem, has been reproduced in S. A. Drake's monograph, and the picture is also given in Bugbee's sketch, and in Coolidge's "Brochure." In the Gentleman's Magazine, Feb., 1790, there is a view of Charlestown and Howe's encampment on the hill, taken after the battle, and in the Massachusetts Magazine, Sept., 1789, is a view of Charles-river Bridge, showing the configuration of Bunker's and Breed's Hills.

The well-known picture which Colonel Trumbull, in 1786, painted of the battle, and of which a key will be found in the New England Historical and Genealogical Register, vol. xv., and of which there is a description in Trumbull's autobiography, gave the command in the redoubt to Putnam, and a subordinate position to Prescott, which the painter is said afterwards to have regretted, as indicating views on the question of command at variance with the truth. A picture by D. M. Carter represents Prescott in command, and this is reproduced in Coolidge's "Brochure." For accounts of the Monument, see Ellis's edition of 1843; Frothingham's "Siege of Boston;" and Wheildon's "Life of Solomon Willard."

THE SIEGE OF BOSTON, JUNE, 1775—MARCH, 1776.

The siege of Boston began with the return of the British troops from Concord on the evening of April 19, 1775, and Putnam fortified Prospect Hill immediately after the battle of Bunker Hill; and after Washington's taking the command, July 3, 1775, the completion of the lines about the town was begun.

The fullest account of the events succeeding the 17th of June will be found in Frothingham's " Siege of Boston," but a general survey of the events will be found in Bancroft and Barry; and popular accounts can be followed in Dawson's " Battles of the United States ; " in E. E. Hale's " One Hundred Years Ago," and in the general histories. Gordon gives details from diaries of the times ; and illustrative matter of contemporary origin is given in Almon's " Remembrancer ; " in Force's " American Archives ; " in Moore's " Diary of the American Revolution." See also the Collections of the Essex Institute, vol. III. ; the diary of General Heath in the camps at Roxbury and Cambridge, in the Proceedings, May, 1859, of the Massachusetts Historical Society.

The letters of Washington, in Sparks's edition. during his stay at Cambridge, are of the utmost importance, as are those of Joseph Reed, his military secretary. See also the autobiography of Col. John Trumbull, who was at this time of Washington's military family, and the life of Dr. John Warren (brother of General Joseph Warren), of the medical staff.

Of the associations of Washington with his head-quarters at Cambridge, see Alexander McKenzie's article in the Atlantic Monthly, July, 1875 ; and Charles Deane's paper in the Proceedings of the Massachusetts Historical Society, Sept., 1872 ; see also June, 1858. In this connection see Rev. Dr. Peabody's oration at Cambridge, July 3, 1875, and the poem " Under the Great Elm," by James Russell Lowell, in the Atlantic Monthly, Aug., 1875. Also much connected with the Cambridge centre, and the left wing, can be learned from Drake's " Middlesex ; " and for the whole line, in Lossing's " Fieldbook."

Various diaries and letters of contemporaries, written during this interval, have been printed, like that of Dr. Belknap, in the Cambridge Camp, Oct., 1775, etc., in Proceedings, June, 1858, of the Massachusetts Historical Society; that of Paul Lunt, in the Cambridge Camp, May 10 to Dec. 23, 1775, in the same, Feb., 1872; that of Ezekiel Price, in the same, Nov., 1863; the Andrews papers in the same Proceedings, July, 1865; the diary of Aaron Wright, in the Boston Transcript, April 11, 1862; a diary in the Historical Magazine, Oct., 1864; letters, which had been used by Frothingham, but were not printed in full till they appeared in the New England Historical and Genealogical Register, April, 1857; and letters in the Proceedings of the Massachusetts Historical Society, June, 1873; in the American Historical Record, Dec., 1872.

On the evacuation in March, 1776, there are letters in the New England Historical and Genealogical Register, VIII., p. 231, etc.; in the Proceedings of the Massachusetts Historical Society, 1858. Dawson, in his "Battles," gives Howe's despatch from Nantasket Roads, March 21, 1776; and Washington's despatch of March 19, 1776.

The appearance of Boston at this time can be judged of from a plate representing the landing of the British troops to garrison the place in 1768, by Paul Revere, which is reproduced in Rand, Avery & Co.'s "Bunker Hill Centennial." There is a view of the harbor and town in the Pennsylvania Magazine, June, 1773; a description with a view in the Columbian Magazine, Dec., 1787; and one of the town from Breed's Hill in the Massachusetts Magazine, June, 1791; and in July, 1793, a large view of the Old State House, and for another see Aug., 1791; in July, 1789, one of the Hancock House; in March, 1789, one of Faneuil Hall, — all showing the aspects of revolutionary Boston. A view showing Dorchester Heights is in the number for Nov., 1790; and another of Boston from those heights, in 1774, is copied from a contemporary English print in Lossing's "Field-book," I., p. 512.

Descriptions of the town and its society at a little later date will be found in the letters of Anburey, who was one of Burgoyne's officers, quartered at Cambridge in 1777; in Abbé Robin, a chaplain of Rochambeau, in 1781, whose account is quoted by Shurtleff, and translated in the Historical Magazine, Aug., 1862; and in Chastellux, 1782, also quoted in Shurtleff's "Description of Boston."

BATTLE OF BUNKER HILL.   173

There is a view of Gage's lines on Boston Neck in Frothingham, from a print published in 1777, and a plan of them in Force's "American Archives," and an original plan reproduced in the "Centennial Graphic." See also Pennsylvania Magazine, Aug., 1775, for Gage's lines. A plan of the fort erected by the British on Bunker Hill proper is given in Frothingham's "Siege," from one published in London, in 1781.

Shurtleff, in his "Description of Boston," ch. 6, gives a chapter to the enumeration of maps of the town and its harbor, some of which are of interest in understanding the circuit of fortifications erected by the provincial forces at this time. The best for consultation is the eclectic map given by Frothingham, p. 91. See also that in Force, vol. III., and the military maps in Marshall's "Washington," Sparks's "Washington," reproduced by Guizot, Lossing's "Field-book," etc.

For contemporary maps, that in vol. I. of Almon's "Remembrancer," drawn at Boston in June, 1775, shows for the field of battle, the words "Breed's Pasture," which accords with the belief that that eminence was not known as Breed's *Hill*, till after the battle. It is not otherwise very accurate.

The Gentleman's Magazine, Jan., 1775, gave a chart of the town and harbor.

The Pennsylvania Magazine, July, 1775, gave a plan of Boston, with a side-sketch of the lines about the town, which has been reproduced in Moore's "Ballad History," and in the Centennial Memorials of Rand, Avery & Co., of George A. Coolidge, etc. Col. Trumbull, in his autobiography, gave a map of the lines made by himself in Sept., 1775.

A large map of the town, with surrounding country and harbor, after Samuel Holland's surveys, was published by Des Barres in London, Aug. 5, 1775. It shows no fortifications except those at Copp's Hill and on the Neck. A colored copy of this is in the Boston Public Library, as is also a French map, 1780 : "Carte particulière du Havre de Boston, réduite de la carte anglaise de Des Barres." The 1775 plate of Des Barres, without change of date, but nevertheless with changes in some parts, and with the various fortifications of the siege delineated, was published again in 1780–83, in the "American Neptune," and it was from the Hon. Richard Frothingham's copy of this that the reproduction in Shurtleff's "Description of Boston" was made in 1870.

Faden's map of Boston, with the intrenchment of 1775, based on the observations of Page in 1775, was published, London, Oct. 1, 1777, and in a later edition, Oct., 1778, and it has been fac-similed in Frothingham's "Siege."

Roman's map of "The Seat of Civil War in America," 1775, has a rude view of the lines on Boston Neck, and a plan of Boston and its environs.

In 1776 there was published by Beaurain, at Paris, a "Carte du Port et Havre de Boston," which is copied from a British plan, and has in a vignette the earliest known printed representation of the Pine-tree banner. (This vignette is copied by Frothingham, who calls the map "curious but not correct.") There is also a German edition of the same.

In 1777 was published Henry Pelham's map of Boston and environs, which is called "the most accurate" of all. It was published in London, June 2, 1777, shows the military lines, and has been reproduced in Moore's "Diary of the Revolution," and in Drake's "Landmarks."

In 1777, Faden published in London a plan of Boston and vicinity, showing the "rebel works," and based on Page's and Montresor's observations.

The earliest of the eclectic maps, and the one followed by later authorities in assigning the location of the military lines, was that given by Gordon in his history, who took Page's for the town, and Pelham's for the country.

www.ingramcontent.com/pod-product-compliance
Lightning Source LLC
Chambersburg PA
CBHW020250170426

43202CB00008B/309